ABOVE GROUND

Gene Jelks Journey Out of The Woods Back Into The Kingdom Of God

JON NELSON

Above Ground
Gene Jelks Journey Out of The Woods Back Into The Kingdom Of God
by Jon Nelson

Printed in the United States of America.
Edited by Nathan Turner

ISBN 9781498427524

www.xulonpress.com

FOREWORD

"I have been fortunate enough to be with Gene in two distinct parts of his life...

The first was when he was a 16, 17, and 18-year-old young man who expressed a desire to play football in Tuscaloosa and then filled out that dream as a true freshman at the University of Alabama. I saw him continually reinforce his drive to be the best he could be on and off the field.

Everyone knows, in some form or fashion, what happened when the dynamic changed for him in school. But a lot of us never knew the depths of his despair until the pages that will follow mine.

When Gene decided to come "out of the woods," as it were, a lot of the University of Alabama family that was walking with him every step of the way in school is joining him now as he makes his comeback.

It takes us a while, sometimes, to find our way when we are lost. Gene is finding his way and I could not be more proud of him as he faces the demons of his past and works toward a successful present-being a man that we all can be proud of...

I have met both Genes...

I know both Genes...

And you should, too..."

Coach Ray Perkins

ACKNOWLEDGEMENTS

From Gene:

To my mother, Doris A. Jelks, my father Dan A. Jelks, sister Audry L. Jelks, brothers Anthony C. Jelks and Dante L. Jelks, niece Ashley Jelks, nephew Antonio Jelks, and daughter Erica McCowan. Aunts, uncles, cousins, and special friends... I can't thank you enough for all of your love and for being the part of my life you are.

To my grandmother, Christene "Mudear" Mostiller Streeters, I thank you for giving me the bible verses- Proverbs 3:5,6 as a little boy growing up. I have worn them around my neck and memorized them in my heart and have never forgotten them during difficult times in my life.

Thank you for keeping our entire family together with God and Love as well as helping to provide for us.

To my best friend, Chester Braggs, you were taken from us all too soon...

And to Regina Campbell, who was there for me when I had nothing and helped me when I needed help. You are like an angel.

From Jon:

To the Outlaws for your faith, you know who you are...

To my family for being there for me all the time- I love you all...

To my Dad, I love you and I miss you- always...

And for my rock, my wife Patty, I am truly blessed to have you as my partner. I cannot express how much I love you and words will always fail me.

TABLE OF CONTENTS

PREAMBLE

Praise God through my fame and shame. God has inspired me to write this book. It took 22 years, but it was worth the wait. Since God gave me a second chance in life, I promised Him that I would surrender my way and will to His perfect plan if he helps me come out of the woods. I wanted to put this book out there to inspire other people and be a blessing to children, to trust, believe, and keep their faith in God- and that God is able to help at your lowest of lows whether we are talking about homelessness, relationships, jobs, family, health, and searching for your next dollar.

God helped me put this book together along with folks like Big Phil, Gil Tyree, and Sam Bryant. Special thanks to Regina Campbell and all my Christian mentors- Siran Stacy, Coach Ray Perkins, Kerry Goode, Bishop Steve Smith and First Lady Rita Smith, Gene Lett, Darrin Mayo, David Gregerson, Dave Mack, Leonard Brown, Hoss Johnson, Dr. Michael Wesley, Senior, Brother John Sadler and Bishop Walter Smith who helped support me through some difficult times.

The book shares stories about my life growing up in the Church, clears up the past struggles, coming out of the woods, redemption, and restoration. You will learn about the Brotherhood within the University of Alabama football program and friends and associates throughout the country. I humbly thank and appreciate everyone who contributed and assisted in the book.

All the people that are mentioned in the book are people I know and a few that I know "of." They are all examples of being good people and an inspiration. I have great respect to those who respect is due. I spent a great deal of my life, starting at age 6, dreaming, working and training to become a professional football player. But I had a lot of help from a lot of people along the way, so I want to thank each and every one of you.

You guys have touched my life!

My goals from this moment forward are to be a servant leader, a blessing to others with my testimony and Glorify the Father in Heaven and His son, Jesus.

I am grateful for my family, friends, and everyone who make all of this possible as well as the sponsors for my Christian football camp and those who believe in my Foundation.

Lastly, I thank my mother, Doris A. Jelks one final time…

My mom is the best and strongest woman I know. She prayed and encouraged me to always trust God, believe and wait on Him to deliver me out of my mess. I love you, Mom!

Gene

INTRODUCTION

Hitting "rock bottom" depends on the person, the personal definition, and the time in your life that it happens.

It could be doing something you shouldn't for one more time that you should have in the first place... It could be having something done to you one too many times...

Or it could be just hitting the wall... the point of no return... where all the fight you have mustered up over however long you've been fighting is gone...

Long gone...

You want to call home, but you can't...

You want to reach out to someone who you think loves you and you love back, but you can't...

For whatever the reason deep in your mind...

You...

Just...

Can't...

You want to move, but you can't... almost frozen in place...

Frozen in a place and time where with all your heart, all your soul, and all your mind you want to go back to a simpler time where the headaches don't exist...

The heartaches don't exist...

And you don't have to think about your next minute... much less your next move...

And that next move for Gene Jelks was a life or death move...

And to understand the next move he could make, you have to understand home...

It was about 5 degrees one winter night in Atlanta. I had about four blankets on the ground. I had no food... I mean, it was literally hard cold. My body was tired of walking. I was tired of walking miles and miles and miles for food. Finding food through word of mouth...

Hearing that they were feeding people over here and they were feeding people over there... it took a toll on me. I went from dressing real nice to dressing in hand me downs and bum clothes... not being around educated people that I was used to... not being able to have access to technology. Not having access to free will and food... not having access to a bank account, checking or savings.

That lifestyle got old and weary. Seeing other people walk to and fro and drive their nice cars that I once had. And I no longer had nothing but God. And some times, the adversary had something to say to me- the devil- and I had a choice to make.

It was bitterly cold that winter night in Atlanta, Georgia...

I got up under those blankets and I was shivering and there was a Dumpster by the Atlanta Journal-Constitution offices. That's where the Popeye's restaurant near Underground Atlanta emptied all their food. I kept my ears open and you had to do that on the street to survive... and know where to find food.

I walked down the railroad tracks; it was cold down into the marrow of my bones. I didn't find any food. I just found bones and boxes and went through the trash trying to find some kind of nourishment for my body...

I had no food... No way to call my family... no way for them to come and get me... I thought I was literally gonna die of hypothermia.

I got up under those covers and I said 'God, you know my heart. I have entertained the world, my family, and the University of Alabama.' Because God gave me that talent to help me in this situation...

I told him "I gave you my heart, my mind, and my soul- just send me somebody because I was hungry. I was scared. And I didn't know what else to do so I cried out to him. With all my

heart and the way he made me out of my mother's womb. And I asked him to feed me, send somebody to me, and send me a sign.

I cried out...

"I'll do whatever you want me to do —no excuses- not religion, not Christianity, none of that." I said, "Speak to me."

A week later I was still homeless, but he answered my prayer. Some railroad track police officers showed up that night. Flashed their lights at me and they said, 'Do you have some ID?' I said yes, I had just gotten off work. I hustled at a restaurant washing dishes and hadn't gotten paid yet. I was still waiting to get my first check in. I know they weren't from God. They were looking for people who

were running scams. All I remember was that it was so cold. They said that I could stay down at the railroad tracks and tell them information... be an informant...

And I said, "No." I told them that they can just go ahead and arrest me for trespassing...

I have nowhere to go...

Chapter 1:

THE EARLY YEARS

Gadsden, Alabama, has a 3-city population of just under 37,000 with a metropolitan reach of just over 104,000. The town was brought up on the Coosa River as one of the most influential seaports in the state- home to as much riverboat traffic in the 20th century as Mobile was for sea traffic. The home of the Goodyear Tire and Rubber Company and Republic Steel plants in the state went from a population of 55,000 at its peak in the 1950's to having the designation of being "one of the seven worst cities to live in" when Rand McNally came knocking in 1989, due to the collapse of those industries in following decades.

The 60-40 percentage of black-to-white led to serious segregation issues–as in most of the South in the 1960's–in this community an hour northeast of Birmingham up Highway 11. Gadsden would be the center of attention for key events in the civil rights movement in the early part of the decade...

Sit-ins were all over the South as one of the forms of protest against segregationist practices. In 1960, Joseph Faulkner, a union steelworker, and two friends- George Woods and Arthur Young- were arrested for defying segregation by sitting in the front rows of a bus. They formed the East Gadsden Brotherhood which built a movement with sit-ins, protests, and mass meetings led by Rev. L.A. Warren and Rev. H.J. Hoyt.

William Lewis Moore was a Baltimore, Maryland postal worker and a member of CORE- the Congress of Racial Equality. In the early 1960s, Moore decided he would go on three separate protests on his own where he marched to a state capital to hand-deliver letters he had written denouncing racial segregation.

His first march was to Annapolis, Maryland. His second march was to the White House, around the same time that Martin Luther King, Jr. was being released from the Birmingham jail. The letter, meant for President Kennedy told him that his intent was for his third march to be to Jackson, Mississippi from Chattanooga, Tennessee. He supposedly asked of Kennedy: "If I may deliver any letters from you to those on my line of travel, I would be most happy to do so."

His third letter was meant for Mississippi Governor Ross Barnett urging him to accept integration. Moore was wearing sandwich board signs that had the phrase "Equal rights for all & Mississippi or Bust" on them. On April 23, 1963, about 70 miles into his march near the town of Attalla, Moore was interviewed as he walked along U.S. Highway 11 by both Charlie Hicks, a reporter from WGAD-AM in Gadsden, Alabama, and a reporter from the Chattanooga Daily Times newspaper. The radio station had received an anonymous phone tip about Moore's activity and went to file a story for their evening newscast. In the interview Moore had with Hicks, he said that "It's about time we've got rid of the black eye we've got when it comes to race relations. I believe the governor's wrong when he says that all Mississippians want segregation." After his interview, Hicks offered to drive Moore to a motel for his own safety, but he was going to keep walking and keep his pledge.

Moore would then face another 30 minutes in a car with Alabama investigator, Roy McDowell, who wanted to know what he was up to and McDowell would also try to encourage Moore to take off his sandwich boards so as to not bring more attention to himself than he already had done. The law officer was unsuccessful in getting Moore to stop his walk, but he did get him to promise he would stop for the night at a truck stop three miles down the road.

Moore would never get to the truck stop...

In the small town of Keener, Moore's body was discovered with two gunshot wounds in the head from the discharge of a .22.

After Moore's death, President Kennedy had his aides try and find the letter that Moore left him on his second march for integration. Lee White, Kennedy's press aide, encouraged the president to directly address Alabama Governor George Wallace, who had referred to the federal government as an "imperialist invader."

Kennedy said, as relayed in Mary Stanton's book, "Freedom Walk: Mississippi or Bust":

"...we had an outrageous crime, from all accounts in the state of Alabama, in the shooting of the postman who was attempting in a very traditional way to dramatize the plight of some of our citizens being harassed on the road. We have offered the services of the FBI in the solution of the crime."

Governor Wallace grudgingly offered a $1,000 reward in the solving of the crime against Moore. Moore's efforts even made content for an editorial in the New York Post two days after his murder where it was said that "... he (meaning Moore) spent his life tugging at the world's coat sleeve. When it last began to listen, William Moore was gone."

A man by the name of Floyd Simpson owned the gun that was involved in the Moore shooting. Simpson and a friend and fellow postman, Gaddis Killian, had argued with Moore earlier that day during his walk north of town. But there were no charges filed in the Moore case, further igniting the community.

After the murder, the East Gadsden Brotherhood started boycotting white merchants in mid-June of 1963 and began protesting and marching just like what was going on an hour down the road. CORE, the Student Nonviolent Coordinating Committee (SNCC) and the Southern Christian Leadership Conference (SCLC) all sent representatives to help organize any efforts to further the town protests.

Al Lingo, the commander of the expanded Alabama State Troopers under Governor Wallace, was one who believed that clubs, cattle prods, mass beatings, and intimidation could drive blacks into an attitude of submission and compliance. The cattle prod was a new weapon for Lingo and his troopers by 1963 as they could deliver a battery-powered shock of up to 24 volts to discipline protesters. On June 18th, hundreds were arrested for protesting. The next evening, hundreds more followed in their place on the steps of the Etowah County courthouse to protest the previous day. State troopers went after the second group, as documented by CORE field secretary William "Meatball" Douthard writing about what he saw from his jail-cell window in the Liberal News for their February-March 1965 newsletter:

Vividly I remember the night of June 19, when over 500 Negroes, men, women, and children, assembled on the grounds of the County Courthouse and jail, to hold a vigil of prayer in protest of the arrest of some 600 students and adults the previous day. While watching from my top floor cell, I saw over 300 law officers of the city, county and state surround the protesters and begin their systematic beating of all. As the Negroes broke and ran they were chased on foot and in cars, overtaken and beaten again.

Leaving jail on bond, I resumed my job as director of demonstrations. By this time the pattern of resistance had formed and we were able to anticipate actions by the city and state authorities. What we didn't expect was the continuous beatings.

Protests kept going for the next six weeks... as did the beatings...

On August 3rd, a mass march led by Rev L.A. Warren was attacked by troopers. The marchers were arrested, beaten and attacked with cattle prods on the way to jail. The women were held in the Gadsden city jail while the men were placed in the Etowah County Jail- to the point of overflowing both. Anyone arrested that wasn't able to be processed in either jail was lined up on the street two-by-two.

Colonel Lingo was reported to have yelled, "Move 'em out!"

The prisoners were moved, with clubs and cattle prods, down to the Gadsden Coliseum- almost two miles away from the jails. Lingo supposedly was trying to get demonstrators to be more violent with the police on hand- goading them into more violence giving his troopers the chance to escalate the proceedings, but Reverend Warren told the arresting officers:

"We won't turn around."

The situation got worse for the protesters that were on their forced march...

From the Civil Rights Movement's Veterans website, crmvet.org:

At the Coliseum the protesters are ordered to lie down. Again many are beaten. The prisoners are forced aboard big 18-wheel cattle trucks. The convoy of cattle trucks and squad cars heads north on

Hiway 431, then halts at an open field. The Ku Klux Klan is holding a rally, complete with white hoods and a burning cross. The troopers laugh, and threaten the prisoners with KKK lynchings and mutilations. Eventually the convoy proceeds to an isolated, semi-abandoned, rural prison camp where the Black freedom fighters are forced to endure six days of inedible food, sleeping on damp concrete floors, and more beatings before the Movement can locate and bail them out.

Though the savage brutality of the State Troopers does manage to temporarily quell the protests in Gadsden, Lingo's broader strategy of suppressing the Alabama freedom movement fails.

Demonstrations, integration lawsuits, and other forms of resistance increase around the state — Tuscaloosa, Huntsville, Selma, Montgomery, Tuskegee, Mobile, Anniston, and elsewhere. And from the trial of one of those arrested in Gadsden — CORE field secretary Mary Hamilton — grows a Supreme Court victory in what becomes known as the "Miss Mary" Case, a victory that changes courtroom behavior nation-wide and that endures to this day.

The Goodyear Plant in Gadsden

The Jelks family grew up in and around all of that civil rights history, activity, and fear. They had to face it full bore at points in their lives as they raised their kids in Gadsden. Doris and Dan Jelks raised a blue-collar family of four kids- Gene, Dante, Anthony, and their only daughter, Audry. Doris worked with the General Electric and Goodyear plants while Dan worked over at Republic Steel.

The Jelks family grew up poor, admittedly. Though they didn't have much, there were no complaints.

According to Gene, "We were poor but you couldn't tell. Each Easter we got a new suit and my sister got her new dress. We would take pictures, and had to do an Easter speech. I was kinda fearful in front of an audience of adults. All my brothers and I got Easter buckets and my sister was the one who got an Easter basket. I just wanted to get the chocolate at the end of the day and I'm good.

"We had plenty of food. My grandmother was a head cook at an all-white school, and she would bring home leftovers. She would share with the neighbors' kids because she would bring home more than we could even eat ourselves. I just remember 'love' and 'being loved.' My mother provided a lot of love. My Grandmother, my aunts, and uncle-they were all loving people. But our whole family didn't stay in Gadsden as I grew up. One aunt went out west to make a better living and she would always help my mom. People provided for us.

"I remember how tired my mom used to be working 2nd and 3rd shift, and she even took a nightclub job cooking for extra money. There was a little closet section that they would put me and my brother in until she got off work to keep us safe and cared after."

So, that meant that if you wanted to make any kind of a living in black Gadsden, you had to find other ways to supplement your life off minimal wages. For Gene, it meant he could use his hands- with some help.

"I made my money using my grandmother's tools and helping other people fix things. I remember one thing we did to pass the time when I wasn't working. All the kids in the neighborhood made boats with sticks and wanted to see what could float down the river the furthest.

"All of that motivated me to want to be a supreme or elite, world-class athlete when I discovered that I had that kind of talent. As I grew up, I remember at the age of 6 having a dream," Gene says. "I was watching television on a black and white in our house and I would get to watch the Miami Dolphins. I dreamed as a little kid of playing for Don Shula.

"At the age of 6, I had a dog, Ruffie, a German Shepherd. We took a picture. I got a Dolphins bandana and I put it on the dog. I also got a Dolphins sweatshirt and wore it all the time."

Like many in the South, the Jelks family was also rooted in their religious beliefs. There was time always set aside for church- more than one day a week, more than one service a week.

No exceptions...

"All we had was church," Gene continues. "We were very poor. We had cars and we would get the chance to go shopping, though. My mom raised us in the church in Gadsden. But, we had to go to church sun up to sun down. Occasionally, we would go to relatives' houses to visit. But that was about it when it came to any kind of social life. I also remember having to attend church functions for African-Americans. It was just reality."

The Jelks family church in Alabama City, Alabama

That and within a decade of all the talk of William Moore's murder, the Brotherhood, Colonel Lingo, the marching, the abuse, and the protests, nothing had really changed socially.

There are eight active groups affiliated with the Ku Klux Klan in the state of Alabama. And in 1970, the Attorney General of the state of Alabama, Bill Baxley, had reopened the 16th Street Church bombing case in Birmingham from September of 1963. Four girls died in the incident and it is widely thought of as a turning point in the civil rights movement and led to the Civil Rights Act of 1964. Baxley's investigation was addressed in a letter to him where he was told by Grand Dragon Edward R. Fields that the investigation was done for "tactical reasons."

Baxley's response to Fields, in just as official a form in its response, was Fields could kiss his ass.

That kind of verbal jousting would not deter either side from getting their points across. Active membership and sympathetic individuals to the Klan numbered anywhere from 26-to-33,000 according to the Anti-Defamation League, and with a headquarters for the United Klans of America in Tuscaloosa- 123 miles to the southwest, it was easy to form numbers to get their points across in the state of Alabama.

Gadsden and the Jelks family saw their share...

"We experienced the KKK having rallies 500 yards from my home," Gene admitted. "My mom told us that we couldn't leave the yard because the KKK was down the street protesting."

What Gene saw was one thing that impacted him and his upbringing. The other event that happened to him as a boy seems to be an indicator for everything that would drive him- even to this day.

A 1997 study by the U.S. Department of Justice reported that just under 10-percent of all adolescents in the United States have been sexually assaulted. Only 12-percent of all cases are reported to any official and more than 90-percent of all abused children know their perpetrator.

Gene Jelks is one of those statistics... and the act itself brings a vile taste to his mouth and the words he uses to describe what happened.

"I remember as a little boy, a neighbor's older kid molested me," Gene admits. "We were just three houses down from my grandparents' house. I know today that individual had a problem. I remember asking this neighbor a question- if I could have something- I don't remember what. I vaguely remember him saying that if he could do something to me, he'd give it to me. I was, maybe 5 years old...

"I went down on him... I don't even remember if I got what I asked for..."

But Gene never told anyone of that day... and for understandable reasons. The older boy told him not to tell anyone. Gene was traumatized and scared enough as it was and, then, he had that order heaped on top of the stigma that would go with the act in the woods.

"I didn't tell my parents out of fear. I remember thinking 'I don't want to go through procedures.' I have run into this gentleman back in Gadsden to this day. He said he was proud of me doing my ministry. God has put me at peace with it..."

What Gene didn't tell anyone after those encounters was that he really wanted to kill the guy on the spot. Gene would just follow up the conversation with a "Thank You" and move on- and that included the thoughts of killing the gentleman who put all this shame and pain into his heart and soul.

But that begs to ask the questions:

If you've never told anyone, then why not get help...?

And you couldn't even tell your parents...?

Was the event so traumatic... so intimidating... that it had to stay with you and stay inside left to fester and eat away at the person you were to create another person entirely...? Long before you were a person you wanted to be...???

Was this event in the woods, with someone from your own neighborhood that was fairly well known by all, supposed to stay in the woods shielded from all- perhaps, including yourself for the long term...???

"My parents might have asked 'Why didn't you come out with what he did?' He was a neighbor down the block," Gene admits. "He was known, but he was like a big brother. But I didn't know he had this freaky side to him.

"We did it in the woods..."

And that's where the molestation and the abuse stayed... shielded by the woods... shielded by Gene from everyone else to create an injury so deep that it created other injuries along the way.

"I was the first-born in my family. I always felt a void in my spirit," Gene says. "I wanted a big brother or sister, and I always seemed to look to older guys for trust.

"There was a trail next to his house. He asked if I'll come in the woods with him and he said: 'I'm gonna pull out my penis' and he told me to go down on him. It traumatized me, really... I don't remember if he gave what I wanted in the first place to me or not."

The event re-emerged in Gene's mind strongly about 6 years ago. What triggered that? Hearing about child molesters on television. Today's 24-hour, 500-channel-universe gives everyone the chance to catch something on practically any topic across the board. Crime and punishment are dotted across, at least, half a dozen channels on their own and fill up a few spaces on the TV Guide by themselves. Gene was watching TV in one of those situations and could identify with those who were abused, left alone, left in a corner, left to think about what to do and what could be done—if anything.

That this neighbor made Gene pull his penis out of his pants, give him oral sex, and not tell anyone puts him in a silent majority of those who have suffered as children—forced to accept it as part of your own fabric as you grow old.

"I guess I was shocked or embarrassed," Gene says. "I guess that's why I didn't reveal it to my family. The guy was in the military. He mentioned that to me, but I was angry about it as I grew older. I wanted to do something, but I didn't know what I could actually do as an adult. I think the statute of limitations on something like that is long gone. Here he is in Gadsden telling me and other people how I was in ministry, and that he could see the glow of glory on me, and that he was proud of me? I was thinking to myself, '*What is that all about...?* All I said was 'Okay, thank you...' and moved on. I ran into him again at a high school reunion—and after seeing him that first time, I really did have a fear of going back. He said 'Do you know who I am?' I said 'Yes, I do,' and I ran out of the building. I ran into him a third time when my mother took sick. He was complimenting me on the beginning of my ministry. I said thank you, and I said that just being cordial. He also said that he'd communicate with me later. He even said, on the record, that he's a preacher now, and that he used to sleep with a lot of women, and got shot at by their husbands. I don't know if he's forgotten what happened between us in his mind. I just remember going down on him. Mentally, I didn't want to stay there when we were in the woods. I just want to forget about it."

But it's obvious to anyone who is around Gene that, while there's still that ear-to-ear grin that can be seen when someone tells a joke or a story, and the belly laugh that comes with the eyes that shine and squint looking with you and through you at the same time, there's a lot of hurt there.

And that's only one direction where the hurt is coming from.

Hurt and emotional trauma can go in one of two directions. It can be used as a motivator, or as a weight to keep you from pursuing a goal or a dream. Gene chose to turn it into the former, and he found a location and an outlet for it. He would use it as a way to showcase his skills and try and leave Gadsden, the woods, the abuse, and the way of life behind—way behind, and try to catch him.

Chapter 2:

RUN, YOUNG MAN, RUN...

"I first gravitated to football at 6. I was hooked," Gene admits. His pace quickens as he talks like he's going through plays in his head that only he knows how to execute.

"I saw eleven guys on each side of the ball- and just the physical contact that was there- everyone can tell you I was focused on football. I went to bed and even slept with a football. I didn't know if I had the skills, I just had to develop them."

Gene's mother would still be heavily involved in the church, and his father would be out of the house doing other things. But Gene will be the first to tell you that football was that first step in trying to escape, or even get some kind of release from what happened in the woods. It was a way to suppress all the anger and give him an outlet for his anger and betrayal from someone so close to him in his old neighborhood.

"It was a motivation... an outlet... from the most traumatizing thing I've experienced," he admits.

"The Bible says to look at it as an experience to be a voice, and be anxious, but it wasn't time to be that voice. You have to accept and deal with it. It didn't steal my spirit or soul. But what football gave me was an escape for me to go forward, to have an outlet for all of my anger, and a place to be free... to be what you wanted to be... it was freedom..."

At the age of 6, Gene played only offense on a team in the Drake Pee-Wee league. Jackie Ragland was his first head coach. And even in his elementary school years at that young an age, Ragland saw something in Gene:

"Gene must have been maybe in the 3rd or 4th grade, and he wanted to play pee-wee ball," his first coach, Jackie Ragland, remembers. "He wasn't that big, he was kinda small. I knew his father because we were in school together. All I know was that one of his cousins could run fast. When his father brought him out, Gene was a little fella, a little frightened, but we gave him the ball, and went through the other drills like all the other kids.

"But when we gave him the ball, he took off and left everybody.

"It was almost like there wasn't anybody on the other team around to tackle him."

Coach Ragland would tell Gene that he was just a frightened little kid and that was the reason nobody could catch him.

In retrospect, Ragland may not even know just how right he is.

The older kids almost couldn't catch Gene- right off the bat, and Ragland knew that there was some exceptional talent he had at running back. When Gene's team started on offense- even if they were on their own one-yard line, Gene would get the ball.

And, like most coaches who have a special player, Ragland fought those questions they all face- regardless of level.

How much do I play Gene...?

Knowing his team could score every time out there if they hand him the ball...?

How much is too much...?

How much is considered running up the score and how much is considered getting his players their reps so they can win...?

But not embarrass the opposition at the same time...

Ragland would face that question when he got to it- and not a moment before...

"I had to not give him the ball because every time we gave him the ball, he scored a touchdown," Ragland admitted. "It just seemed like he was heads and shoulder above the other guys. I first thought it was just that every other team was weak, but it was just that he was exceptional. And the only way I could hold the score down was by not giving him the ball.

"He was just amazing, really... he started out with an exceptional talent with pee-wee ball. He was always exceptional. Even in middle and high school he was very confident...

"Kinda like his father..."

The way Dan Jelks carried himself was how Gene decided to do it. He was very confident in what he could do. There wasn't a cockiness there, but a confidence in what they could do and who they could be. For Dan, it was being a hard-working man at the plant. For Gene, it was running from one end of the football field to the other and helping his team win. Gene was a good athlete like his dad, and he was a natural when he was handed the football.

Donald Harris, Sr. knew all of the Jelks clan... as far back as the grandparent's limb of the family tree...

They all grew up together in the Black Creek area of Gadsden where it was a 15 minute walk north from 16th Street to Black Creek-since Gene's time in "grammar ball" as he puts it where Gene was fast, quick , and had the speed to make it all happen. But Harris leads on to something that would cause people to take stock in Gene all over again when he was older:

"Gene was a good kid. You could trust him and you knew what was coming out of his mouth was the truth. I counseled at the Central Boys Club when he was 8 or 9 years old. One time they were playing basketball out there on the court and I called 'time out,' and he was the first one to sit down. And then, when it was time to let them back out there, they'd play better basketball.

"You know how there's the good and the bad…?

"The bad wasn't Gene because he was out there playing basketball. He was enjoying himself.

"His family is Christian-hearted folks... and they could sing... all of his relatives could sing. They would all sing gospel.

"He wasn't raised no 'hood rat.'

"He had a Christian background. His mother wasn't going to put up with any of that... "Why do you think he played at Alabama...?

"I think Gene was just a natural," Ragland says. "He had that instinct. He knew where to go, and for him the game was easy to learn. He was always focused, even as a pee-wee player. He caught on real quick and I think he worked hard in trying to find the right way to do things. He was learning the game even as a pee-wee player. He knew what it was about. He would always make good decisions, and he was a natural runner. I think he always wanted to be a running back, and I think he enjoyed running the ball.

"He was a nice guy, a hard-nosed Bill Parcells-like or Mike Ditka-like coach," Gene remembers about his time with Ragland. "He always pushed you to the limit."

But there is also one other thing that Gene carries with him about his time with Ragland- a noise that would always get your attention...

And it was a noise that got your attention...

"There was this ring he had on his hand," Gene remembers as he fiddles with his own right hand.

"He would hit you on the helmet- nothing violent or anything like that. But he would pop you on your helmet..."

Plink!

"You'd know when that ring hit your helmet. It was not abusive or anything like that, because he was a real tall, gentle spirit. He was very caring, and truly outside of my dad and family and friends-he guided me the right way. I have a lot of respect for Jackie."

Plink!

The Jelks neighborhood today in Gadsden

Gene would run for five or six touchdowns a game and everyone seemed surprised at what Gene could do on the football field at such a young age. For a six or seven-year-old kid all the way through elementary school, it was an exciting time. And it was fun for the kids and the adults who got to watch it happen. It gave him the chance to be something he wanted to be...

And something that didn't have anything to do with the woods...

But it still meant that he had to be home by dark and he still had to go to church with his family. Five or six scores meant a lot, but there were still chores and being a part of the Jelks family on a daily basis... a family that was known for its belief in God and following of Him on a daily basis. Doris Jelks was not going to have anything to do with peer pressure or anything like that. It was a family known by its love and respect for God and nothing was going to change that...

Gene called it "strict," but for Doris it was the way...

Someone else saw it, too, from Gene's time in the Central Boys Club- Local Director Eddie Nichols:

The Jelks family house today in Gadsden today

"I saw him out there running in the back of the playground- leaving athletes in the dust," Eddie recalls. "Gene was so involved with sports programs as one of the kids at the Boys Club. Eventually, he was old enough to where he went on sports trips. He was entrenched in all that athletic activity, and he loved it! He had a passion and gift for it. He was dedicated to it.

"He had a phenomenal relationship with his mom- and his relationship was so unique with his mother so involved. It was exciting when you see folks that begin to excel- with all the hard work paying off.

"When the spring came around, I coached him in track, and we had a 400M relay team. He was the fastest, and carried the anchor leg for the team."

Dan Jelks was a big part of his success. He was always with Gene, and was there to teach him not to forget where he came from. His dad kept them focused on not forgetting the relationships they were building, no matter how little or insignificant it seemed.

But, for a while anyway, football wasn't Gene's only sport. George Baker coached Gene in basketball and track. Baker also saw the potential that Ragland saw on the football field in the winter and spring.

"I met him in junior high school 7th grade. He was an athlete, and I knew right off he had potential. It was amazing, and being able to talk to the little kids. Gene was one of the few guys who was on his way up, and we thought the world was Gene's. In the black community, he was one of the gifts but he didn't have anything to give but himself.

"He had the whole town buzzing. Everybody was proud of him and his achievements. I got the chance to watch for home games in the fall, and he was a tremendous athlete. He always had determination."

In Gadsden, there were three high schools for anyone to attend when Gene was growing up- Emma Sansom High, Gadsden High, and Litchfield High School.

Emma Sansom High School opened in 1929 and would close in 2006 as part of the consolidation of the three schools into what is now Gadsden City High School. It was named for a young girl who was credited with helping General Nathan Bedford Forrest to cross Black Creek in Gadsden, to get his troops ahead of Union soldiers that would help in stopping a planned attack on Rome, Georgia during the Civil War in May of 1863.

The "Greatest Band in Dixie" was housed at Emma Sansom and, because of all the awards the group received under band directors Billy "Rip" Reagan, his son Steve Reagan, Boyd McKeown, Pat Morrow, and Russ Waits, Gadsden even gave itself the moniker of "The City of Champions" during their reign.

Emma Sansom's biggest rival was the Gadsden High Tigers. Before the state playoffs came into being in 1966, Gadsden was credited with a mythical state title in 1944- going an undefeated 9-0 on the year. Allegiances with the two schools were set early on in life- much like every other rivalry in the state of Alabama. You were either one way or the other and bragging rights were just as important the other 364 days out of the year that the two didn't play as the one day a year that they did.

The first football game played between the Sansom High School Rebels and Gadsden High School was in September of 1932. Sansom's coach, F.A. Reagan, was a former coach at Gadsden High School and was particularly anxious to promote good feelings between the two schools. Gadsden won the first game between the two and would hold a record of 53-24 over the years of the rivalry that included a handful of Charity Bowl matchups at Murphree Stadium which were played for that exact reason- making sure those in need in and around the town were helped out from 1957-1986.

Litchfield High School's Eagles were the third high school in town, starting in 1957- even catching a state title in 1986. But Jelks would end up going through the middle school system and would be heading toward a track to put him in a purple and gold uniform for Sansom.

"As I progressed, all the coaches had an interest in me, but they talked to my dad," Gene admitted. "They didn't talk to my mom- she was neutral- whatever her kids did, she was supportive. It became very interesting when, as the cycle of my growth and level of competition went up, I began to develop this speed. I had no idea, around the age of 9 or 10, what I had when I played football."

There were two steps to learning high school football in the Emma Sansom track in Gadsden- middle school and high school.

One man would hold Gene's future in his hands before he ended up learning from Alabama legend and Rebels varsity head coach Fred "Buster" Gross- Jerry Pullen, the Emma Sansom middle school coach.

And, when you ask Gene, Pullen almost caused Jelks dreams to stop before they even really got started...

"In Junior High, Pullen would come by and pick us up in his pick-up truck and we would do group things together outside of sports," Gene said. "I remember the upperclassmen in junior high discovered that I had this gift in practice. In 7th Grade, I had my shot...

"I begged Coach Pullen to let me play. I struggled back and forth and I was anxious like a Michael Jordan-type athlete. Every time I asked him if I could play, he said that I would have to wait my turn. There was a yearning inside of me knowing that I was better than every other running back out there.

"I was four grades better than any athlete, but the head coach wouldn't give me the opportunity."

"The kids I coached for the 8th grade and freshman teams were really gung-ho," Pullen remembers. "I would take the kids in PE class and have them box. It was a way to learn about the kids you had playing for you. Gene would mix it up with them, too, now...

"The kids really made something of themselves. Especially, that 9th grade team we had at Sansom. All that activity for guys like Gene and 'Brick' Haley helped them by the time they got to the high school football team. Those kids were tough!"

And for the Sansom program, that was according to Pullen "the ideal scenario." You could find the players that you knew were going to excel on the varsity level early on and keep them in the school system. Pullen had Brick and his teammates in class in 8th grade and ushered them in that way.

"And you could tell Gene was talented back then, too," Pullen says. "It was fun watching them grow and, then, seeing them succeed later. I felt like I had a part in that state championship and the one later on at Valley Head High."

Most coaches are very set in their beliefs. You have to earn your spot and you have to wait your turn. Seniors will have the first opportunity to showcase themselves, because they- like years and years of upperclassmen before them- they have waited their turn. They will have their one opportunity (or two, perhaps, during their junior year in school if the coaching staff really sees something in their athlete), but very rarely would a freshman... God forbid, an 8th grader, because that was just unheard of...

He's too young... He's too small...

He can't handle the rigors of varsity football...

We just "don't do that..."

But, forget Coach Pullen for a second... there was another, more important person that Gene had to get through to reinforce the idea that he was very good at football and needed to be around the sport full time...

That's right...

His mother... but Gene had an idea...

"I told my mom that I wanted to be in the band, just to use them as a scapegoat or something," as he recalls the plan to get onto the football field full-time. "She let me go be with the band and I look at that today as being caring and loving. Really, I just didn't want to go home. She was really supportive in anything I did. I told my mom that I wanted to play in the band. So, what does she do...?

"She saves up and gets this expensive $235 trumpet that I didn't know how to play.

"Ms. Diane Turner was our band teacher – and I discovered that I could do this to find a way to use it and go to football practice. One day, my mother found out I missed band practice. I had begged Ms. Turner to let me out of class to go to football practice. It was in the first week of football practice, that fall, I had been in band maybe a month- and I was trying to juggle both. I mean, the football field was just 300 yards away. I begged her to let me leave early and she did.

"I even recall one game in high school at Murphree Stadium, coach Buster Gross let me suit up in the first half. And, then, at halftime I actually took out my shoulder pads and took off my helmet for halftime, 'played' in the band (he faked it), and in the second half put on my uniform and went back to playing."

And, just so you know, Gene finally did learn how to play the trumpet. But it was just in time to focus on running the ball full-time.

That didn't mean that Gene wasn't letting his feelings with Coach Pullen go. He was always angry at him for not letting him play.

Gene's Junior Year Yearbook Football Photo

And Gene almost quit the game altogether out of frustration...

"In 8th grade for me, I had told high school coaches: Go screw yourself! I actually quit football in the 6th or 7th grade- I thought to myself that I'm better than these guys.

"I quit.

"It was a big mistake. My parents put me back restricted to church and church duties.

"Welcome to the real world, right?' So, I begged Coach Pullen. I said: 'Coach, I made a mistake. I wanna get back on the team.' He said, 'Let me think about it.' He didn't get back to me when I wanted him to. I got angry. He finally came back to me and said, 'Listen to me, son. I'll let you come back. But you're gonna have to earn it. I had to do all kind of exercises, suicides, and practices.

"I was scared. I don't know what he's going to do, I just had to find the courage to commit, and I agreed to his terms. I'll never forget I was so dehydrated. I realized then that you have to be careful with what you say or do because it will come back to haunt you.

I remember running so many laps, doing so many push-ups, and sprints, that I would never ever cross him again like that."

The punishment from Coach Pullen lasted about a week. It was evenings after school and then after practice all over again...but it got Gene back in the game after a rash and impulsive decision that most teenagers are capable of doing when they're teenagers.

"I was accepted back on the team and accepted the role that coach gave me," he admitted. "I played a little quarterback, but I was out of position. I loved returning kicks and punts, but when I was a running back... I was a changed guy on the football field. When I first got the ball, to compete with all that energy that was geared to football... to get to the first level, second, level, and then the end zone...?

"In the first year of high school, I was playing at nickel back, I would come up and give you a fan move or something-nothing too physical. It was just a way to play as a freshman. I told Coach Gross, 'I'm out of position, I can beat any senior or junior you have.' But he denied me that chance. One day in practice, the starting running back hurt his ankle, and that turned out to be my chance that I wanted for so long. I eventually had over a thousand yards, but no touchdowns."

But just because you were on the roster and were practicing, didn't mean people actually believed you...

"In my freshman year, I wanted to leave Biology class and on the intercom, they called for the football team to come out of class," Gene says with a laugh. "You know me... I was only 135 pounds.

"Miss Watkins, my Biology teacher said, 'Son, sit down.'

"I told her I had to go and that I was on the football team, and she wouldn't let me go. I had to get someone to get the head coach to come and get me out of class. She just didn't know. They hadn't discovered me yet. The upperclassmen were more popular."

"I don't really remember that," his head coach, Buster Gross, admits now. "But I could see where that could be true. I do remember having to get him out of class. Not really knowing where he was at..."

In high school, Gene also faced another indignation kids his size would face on a regular basis- he would get beat up... Some kids get beat up for not having the social status of others. Some get beat up because they're smaller and the bully senses another opportunity to put a notch in their belt of artificial success. But for the kid who wore hand-me-downs, tight Levi's blue jeans, a Members Only jacket, and boots... he was on the receiving end for a reason only the "big kid" knows.

"It was just not in my spirit," he says looking back. "I wouldn't do what they wanted me to do. I wasn't the bully of the neighborhood in grades 1-4 and it carried through to my time in high school.

But, like most kids that age, you can only take so much even if fighting isn't in your DNA...

And, one day, Gene had heard enough...

"In Grade 8, it was a kid named Tim Keith," he admits. "You know... when you talk about someone's mother, I'm sorry, you gotta fight. I knocked him down and my Mom asked me later 'Why did you fight?' I said that he said something about you. I never thought I would overcome all of this, but football was an outlet."

An outlet he missed and almost missed out on entirely, but seemingly got back to just in time... His football recognition would be getting bigger as he was getting older...

"My Sophomore year, still, all I had was sports and church," he says. "Maybe, a trip to the skating rink on Sunday in Rainbow City was a bonus. Football was still my escape and an outlet. I knew I could be the best athlete in the city and it started happening. People would come up to you in town and they would tell you that they followed you. It gives you this great feeling."

And, because of all of this attention, Gene knew what his football could do...

"I asked my parents, going into 9th grade, to look at colleges to continue to pursue my dreams of playing for the Miami Dolphins and helping my family. My mom said, at the time, I can't afford to send you to school. And that motivated me that much more. I was the starting tailback, and I go over 1500 yards and 15 TDs- and I didn't know that Harriet Murray, the home economics teacher, was keeping up with the stats."

And back in the 1980's, every football fan was looking at tapes of running backs like Earl Campbell in Houston with the Oilers and all of his power. But, cosmetically, as Campbell ran beautifully there were so many defensive players who tried to get a piece of him (before they were run over) that all they could get was a piece of Campbell's jersey...

The tear away- a running back's best friend...

The tear-away was a cool visual for running backs in the 1970s and 1980s- it was a mental thing for the backs to be seen with their jersey shards flapping in the wind. It meant to them that they were tough and willing to do anything to be a success. Gene wanted to look into those tear away jerseys on his own, but he didn't know that they actually did cost money. Every single time a linebacker or defensive back went after a piece of a jersey, it had to be replaced.

So much for that idea... but his numbers improved and so did everyone's interest in him as a running back.

"My Junior year, I started getting letters... Iowa, Ohio State, UGA," he remembers. "I was just a country boy, and my family didn't have the business mindset to think about the next step at the time.

"We had church, and my dream still was there... it was exciting for the city to see me play. A lot of people were rushing home from work. But the light bulb wasn't on yet for me. I was like 'okay, cool.'

"Then it clicked when I was told I was a great athlete...

"The home ec teacher told me stuff about how well I was doing. I really wasn't going home to give my parents feedback on this. It was amazing. I competed harder. I competed to get better. And I had to put myself in a position to take care of my family- first to go to school, and be able to provide more than what we had, instead of going to the neighbor to borrow a cup of sugar. It all motivated me. It was amazing.

"Every year they gave out this trophy to the best athlete in the city. Coach Gross gave out the trophy at the end of the year. Andre Haley, our star defensive tackle, was a year ahead of me- and coach cancelled the trophy that year."

Coach Gross canceled the trophy that year because they both were so good- one on offense and one on defense- he couldn't give it to either one to exclude the other...

When asked if he remembered that, Haley couldn't recall it as a definite memory, but wasn't surprised when it was brought up:

"Yeah, I could see that as being true that year," he admits.

"He's still our hero," Donald Harris admits. "I'm class of Emma Sansom 1976. He did what we failed to do- he won a championship. He was a one-man gang.

"He was Bo Jackson."

And then, Harris admits to something...

"I'm the first class integration of 1969-1970. When Gene and his teammates came through, it was tight. Salt and pepper playing as one... everything was tight and bonded. That's the way he was raised. In the classroom, He was an A and B student. He wasn't a dummy. He wasn't a hard-headed kid."

That tightness led to more wins and higher numbers for college coaches to look at as he hit his junior season on campus...

"Our home ec teacher told me that my stats were over 2800 yards and 28 touchdowns," Gene remembers. "I started getting attention

Gene as an Emma Sansom Rebel on the sidelines

and I liked that. I knew I was on my way to becoming that 6-year-old's dream even when I was brought up poor. I remembered those days when we got a dime for Sunday school. I had to say a Bible verse and I always came up short because I was always spending it on something else. I got a good chewing out and a good spanking.

"I started getting calls, but it was more fun for me to entertain people in the city. And, believe it or not, I didn't left weights... I ran. I was the only player in 30 years that trained the whole city- and I mean, I ran around the whole city. People blew their horns. I would go into the white community run through there and the hood. There were smaller, restricted subdivisions, and people would be coming out clapping... people would honk their horns. I was the only player in the history of my city to train running the whole city. I was dead tired and walked the rest of the way home when I was done.

Only twenty years after the protests, arrests, and violence, Gene was bringing the town together.

Buster Gross coached in Alabama high school football for 29 seasons before retiring for good after the 1991 season. He started his head coaching career, oddly enough, at Southside-Gadsden in 1959 before stops at Walnut Grove and Arab brought him to Emma Sansom for the 1973 season. He led the team through its most successful era from 1977-1984 with seven region titles in the eight year period. He went to school in Gadsden, but he never felt like he was given a chance at Auburn as a 145-pound football player- even if he has the national championship title ring go prove his time was a success on the Plains. It was an era where you could sign as many as you wanted and the coaches would spend your entire freshman year trying to run as many kids off as they could. Knowing what he went through in high school, college practice was easy to him.

So Coach Gross knew special players when they were sent to him... and knew how to get the best out of them... and he would have played Gene as an 8th grader if he could...

"I couldn't wait to get him there," Gross admits. "He had everything that the best have. He had the speed. He had the movements... everything you need in high school. He came up as a 9th grader and started as a freshman. He was a great person, too. And worked real hard...

Downtown Gadsden today

"We just had a lot of pride. I have a lot of pride in helping him achieve it. By the time he was in junior high, I knew what he was going to do. I was seeing what was coming.

"You could see that Gene loved football, and that he was dedicated. I loved giving the football to him. If I didn't give it to him as much as I did, he might have been one of those kids that peeved around, you know... because you're 'not getting the ball.' Kids around him accepted it- we were to get first downs and, then, touchdowns. They accepted it. Remember, there was a fullback and a halfback doing a lot of blocking for Gene. If they hadn't done their job, he couldn't have done his."

But Buster Gross knew all of his players didn't have a car, and he would get his players for practice.

He showed an interest in his players, too, as he understood they were poor and limited in transportation. He made sure the kids had what they needed to make it day-to-day. On the practice field, he reminded Gene of Lou Holtz.

"It was the hardest work ethic I have ever seen," Gene says. "Gross was a hard-nosed old-school coach. He didn't take no for an answer... he had one goal and one goal only- to produce great athletes and have them go to the next level. I respect him a great deal and am grateful to him."

Gross knew what the talents and abilities of each of his players were and believed in each and every one of them. He was hard on everyone he was in charge of on the football field and pushed them to a level where each player knew they had perfected the play... even if, in Gross' own mind, they hadn't perfected the play. He still would make them do it over and over, because as the saying goes, it's not practice that makes perfect. Perfect practice makes perfect.

"It got to the point with me that I said 'Coach, I'm tired,' " Gene admits. "I didn't know he was getting me ready for the long haul. I really respect him to this day. I can say had it not been for him developing me, knowing me, and conditioning me, whether we're talking about the 7-on-7, or the 1-on-1 drills, I wouldn't have been who I was and I wouldn't be who I am today. He didn't see me as a star, but he knew how to keep everyone else around me to survive. He showed how he cared at the end of the day, without verbalizing, and I am always indebted to him for that.

"I could never run a play right. When it was wrong, it was wrong. And when it was right, it was wrong. But I had to be an example for the younger guys on the team. He was hard-nosed, and no nonsense as a coach."

And you always knew where Gross was on the sidelines during the games, even if you couldn't see where he was at any given time. He was always walking around during games. And if you didn't see Coach Gross pacing beside the white lines, he would always be smoking a cigarette and popping his wrists.

His presence was always felt, heard, and seen...

Every memory Gross has about Gene is good. He never had to get on him, but he might have had to say something- just not to where he was getting on him in front of somebody. Coach Gross also knew Gene had a lot of pride. Team leaders like Larry Rose, Freddie Weygand and the like might have said something to Gene if he needed to be spoken to, but they were his equals and he knew that.

Gene knew where his place on the Sansom team was.

"I was a real conservative coach," Gross admits. "I liked to keep the ball-as a ball possession coach. We did a lot of running. But we did have a good passing game because our running game was so good. We didn't go wild about it. We ran the ball on 1st down to keep the ball away from everybody...

"I guess you could say we played played 'old-timey' football."

Gross admits that the run Sansom had was probably one of the best things that happened to the town and the school at the time. They had big crowds, and for Gross who grew up at Sansom with cross-town rival Gadsden beating them every year for 17 years, it was enjoyable too. It took the team a few years to get to the top, and they were pretty high in the state standings- anywhere from 7th to 2nd in 1983 by the time it was over.

"From '78 to '84 we were 78-7, and had some good football players," Gross says. "I want to think I had a lot to do with it, keeping those kids out there. We went for first downs. First downs lead to touchdowns. I wasn't a big play coach, but Gene was a big play runner. We had a boy like Gene, and we threw it more with Freddie Weygand. Gene, Freddie, and Larry Rose all started for me as freshmen. I don't know if anyone has had that with one team play as many as we did who were freshmen. But, at the same time, you don't win without coaching."

1983 Record (13-1)

August 26th at Glencoe	Win 32-7
September 2nd at Etowah	Win 49-0
September 9th vs. Hartselle	Win 14-13
September 16th vs. Fort Payne	Win 39-6
September 23rd vs. Litchfield	Win 37-10
September 30th vs. Gadsden	Win35-27
October 7th vs. Guntersville	Win 35-0
October 14th at Southside Gadsden	Win 24-14
October 28th vs. Boaz	Win 45-7
November 4th vs. Litchfield	Win 30-16 (Charity Bowl)

Playoffs

November 11th at Alexandria	Win 41-0
November 18th vs. Gardendale	Win 20-14
November 25th at Colbert County	Win 23-20
December 2nd at Escambia County	Loss 0-14

"Half your competition was city teams and big rivals," Gross continues. "It's not hard to get up for them. I credit my assistants for that. The kids were ready to play. What I remember more than anything is that we lost four of those games in the state playoffs. It says a lot for the kids and says a lot for the coaches. Our biggest disappointment, obviously, was- not winning in '83. We had injuries with three or four players in the finals. When you lose one or two, it's bad enough, but losing three or four was tough. Freddie Weygand was a great receiver for us and he was injured. He played, but he wasn't 100-percent.

But that set the team up for the run in 1984... and coaches know the buttons to push with their talented kids- especially with so much on the line and so much promise coming to the field every Friday night.

For Gross handling Gene, it was as simple as pulling him aside...

"I remember a few times, not embarrassing him in front of the kids," Gross says. "It would be something like, 'Hey, you know I'll kick your ass,' and that's all he needed. If a great football player gets belittled in front of other players it either helps or hurts. It's different to a player. With me, Gene was just part of the team. He had that God-given ability, but he was part of the team."

1984 Season (15-0, State Champs)

August 31st at Albertville	Win 28-8
September 7th vs. Litchfield	Win 34-6
September 14th at Colbert County	Win 18—15
September 21st at Anniston	Win 41-6
September 28th vs. Etowah	Win 27-0
October 5th at Fultondale	Win 41-0
October 12th vs. Talladega	Win 41-7
October 19th at Etowah	Win 46-0
October 26th at Gadsden	Win 21-15
November 1st vs. Southside-Gadsden	Win 7-0

Playoffs

November 9th vs. Guntersville	Win 42-0
November 16th at Gadsden	Win 27-25
November 23rd vs. Colbert County	Win 10-7
November 30th at Gardendale	Win 7-6
December 7th vs. Greenville	Win 10-7 (OT)

And they had to beat arch-rival Gadsden twice in a four week period just to get to the third round of the playoffs...

Murphree Stadium in Gadsden- the home of the Emma Sansom Rebels

"Gadsden was a real good football team and they were our big rival," Gross says. "Our kids had become used to that. It might have had a lot to do with that. We had played a better schedule and closer ball games, and I think it gave us an edge. If we hadn't beaten them, they would have won state that year, I'm sure."

"It was so competitive. It was so intense from a high level emotion-wise," Gene agrees. "It was one of the most exciting games ever in the regular season, and we had to play them 3 weeks later in the playoffs. Scoop Guyton, Gadsden's star running back and I, we competed all night back and forth. It was a historical year for Sansom playing Gadsden High back to back like that. And 30 years later, people still talk about this."

"I scored twice in less in a minute on a fumble. A lot of games, I can't recall," but ask Gene about a game against Gadsden and he remembers, pretty much anything you ask. "The playoff game was one of the most exciting, competitive games I've ever played in.- They were looking for revenge. Guyton got hit so hard on one play by our defense. They knocked him 10 yards back and he still scored. I scored for us on the next time down the field. It was a battle all night. A lot of people in Gadsden say Guyton was juiced up, and that he was supposed to have a concussion or something. How do you get backed up and still come forward the way he did..? It was the most exciting game on a high school level that I have ever been around."

But they still had a way to go for that state title they missed out on as juniors...

The rivalry meant more to Gross with Gadsden and it dates back to his time in 9th grade where he was supposed to go to Gadsden, but rode the bus every morning to Sansom. He had made good friends with the Gadsden bunch and was living over there with them on that side of town.

But...

"It was a bigger thing to me than other places because of that," Gross admits. "It made me work harder in playing and coaching."

The time that people remember for one reason or another? It was a drive where Sansom had to score to send the game into overtime or win to face Greenville in the finals. And all those freshmen were now upperclassmen, knew what they needed to do and how it needed to be done.

Buster Gross' play-calling would be as it always was... first downs leading to touchdowns...

"They (Gardendale) made a bunch of first downs, but our defense stopped them late... I remember the play we stopped them... if they had made a first, they would have beaten us. But our kids made the first down, drove on down and scored.

Down 6-0 to Gardendale, late in the 4th quarter in the state semi-finals, though, coach and players got together for one of those "drives for the ages." It's one of those drives you see on the highlight reels all the time.

And, then, Gross laughs...

"If we were running the ball, Gene got it probably on every play."

If you look at the tape, Gross isn't far from the truth...

"I can remember we pitched the ball to Jelks every time. He was a boy you could depend on. He loved having the ball in his hands and was giving you everything he had."

Gardendale tried to slow him down. They keyed on him all night long...

Alan Pridmore, in his first season coaching for the Rockets, hadn't really been challenged in all of the games up to that point. Only once was a game-winning margin closer than nine points and that was in a week six at Dora. Their playoff wins were by margins of 10 over Oxford, 19 over Jacksonville, and 22 at Wenonah. QB Marty Uptain threw to All-South wide receiver Roderick Green while Paul Maxwell and Willie Wyatt ran the defense that only gave up a little over six-and-a-half points per game on the average. Gene, admittedly, had no confidence in his own game that cold and wet night where he fought for every yard he could get.

"I was tired and everybody depended on me," Jelks admits. "I took so much punishment that I wanted to be taken out of the game.

This was the drive that was Sansom's last shot at getting to a state title...

At the 14-yard line, the call was for a dive play straight up the middle...

Coach Gross called time out...

The coaches said in the huddle that they were going to double-down on Willie Wyatt and Gene was going to run straight in the end zone. Walter Smith, the left guard, told anyone who would listen that Gene was tired and had no more energy.

It didn't matter...

The offensive line gave him instructions as to what to do...

"I said I can't get the five yards," Gene said to the other ten guys around him. "One of the linemen, Walter Smith, squeezed my hand so hard that it hurt. And he said, 'Tight, we're gonna secure a hole for you and you're gonna run right up our butt. We guarantee you that you'll score.'"

Depending on the angle of the tape and which media report you watch, read, or listen to about the game, the down and distance were either fourth and five from the Gardendale five or fourth and 7 from the Gardendale seven.

"And our saying was 'Gardendale tried and Gardendale died.' They all told me, 'Do exactly what I tell you to do' and I did. If it hadn't been for the offensive line, the fullback, and Walter Smith squeezing my hand, I wouldn't have scored." That night I gave the offensive line and Walter Smith the credit.

"I didn't believe in that play. They did."

Gene and his Sansom teammates had never faced a team that was so disciplined on defense. It was like facing the Pittsburgh Steelers' "Steel Curtain." Gene, the Miami Dolphins fan who knew all about the Steelers growing up, didn't believe in getting that five yards.

Gene scored off left tackle in the game's waning moments for the win and the trip to the last game you could play in a year. Sansom would beat Greenville in overtime for the title in 1984.

But, unlike the Gadsden games, if you ask Gene about the time he wins a ring...??? He just remembers a few things...

"That Overtime...? It was cold. I had a charley horse and sore shoulders. I was ready to call it quits all again. You know, a little 155-pound body is only designed to take so much. That '84 team...? We had less talent, but we stuck to the game plan, we trusted each other, and we had unity.

"15-0 had never been done at my high school," he said knowing the significance of the feat. "At the age of 6, it was predestined to be.

"My mother was on the booster club, and everybody in Gadsden was happy. It unified the city and that, looking back, was the most important thing I have gotten out of that time I spent in high school. It brought the races together, and connected people on a common day. I can say now, with a great deal of certainty, that I'm still being remembered 30 years later. What we as a team – and what I accomplished by asking the coaches to play, when I got the opportunity, it showed on that day.

"I was grateful and proud to be a part of a group of guys that could take the team 15-0."

Guys like Kenny Malone who Gene voted team captain instead of himself. Everyone voted Gene captain, but Gene didn't care about that kind of recognition.

Guys like Larry Rose who helped paved the way in more ways than one... on the field or off...

Offensive teammates like Rich Dobbs and Scott Hilton- whose spirits defined the word "inspirational" in high school... and meant more to Gene than they'll ever know. Their spirits were peace and humility in a time of great turmoil.

Halfback Timothy Merriweather- who is now an ordained minister in Texas. He was as mean as a rattlesnake, but his inner strength helped Gene as a teammate. Merriweather took a lot of punishment blocking for him, and eventually would go to theological school even after failing a failing a grade."

Andy Watts, who developed into a quarterback, after he had to build his mechanics from the ground up.

The friendly battle with Freddie Weygand, where the whole team was concerned about: "Who was the fastest?" Was it Freddie or Gene...? Gene or Freddie...? One day, the coaches decided it was time. The two of them went 100 yards, and Freddie crossed first.

"What's the saying...? White men can't jump...?" Gene asks with a laugh. "Well, white men can run. I was thoroughly convinced Freddie was who he was. Especially, when we were facing each other..."

"Freddie might have been a little bit faster," Coach Gross admits. "If you line them up and run, one might win one first time, one wins the next time. Gene had the speed plus cutting movements that made him. And he was, probably, a greater asset than Freddie. Freddie will catch it 15 times a game and Gene will get the hand-off 30. Having Freddie helped Gene run in our offense, too, with the threat of the pass we had. Defenses had to back off of Gene, but both were great."

"The year before was a sad day," Gross continues. "I have had teams when they voted on number one and number two. When you win 15 games, no one can take it away from you. The year before, it was 13-0 and we didn't get the 14th. I think we had the better team the year when we came in second with Gene and Freddie. It was a better all-around team the year before, but it benefited us for the '84 season losing the one year before...

"The year before by us not putting points on the board, got us ready for next year...

"It was a great run. We won a lot of close games, and in the 1984 season, we won 8 games by a touchdown or less. It says a lot about our kids- that they were good enough to beat everybody. They had to win five games in the playoffs, and they played the best for five straight weeks.

"I'm amazed at what those kids did."

And one guy who would see the impact Gene had over his high school years was the guy who owned the local convenience store- Toney Tolbert.

Tolbert runs two businesses today on Tuscaloosa Avenue- the Beverage and Variety Store and the Jewelry and Pawn right next door.

Every high school kid in every town that they grew up in remembers who they hung out with and where...

For the Emma Sansom kids, it was Tolbert's...

And, like most convenience stores, you were probably asked to contribute to the local little league association- even, maybe, get the name of your business on the back of a team's jersey or have a sign advertising the business on an outfield wall or a sideline fence.

"I think Gene was a Mountain Ram, in a little league for little boys," Toney recalls. "I had a lot of boys in the 80's. I had a wall of accomplishments for everyone in this town...

"Gene had a rough upbringing. His real dad, Eugene Murphy, was my classmate at school. And the guy who married Gene's mother, Dan, raised Gene.

"He was a little running dude with the Mountain Rams, and then went to Samson. Freddie Weygand, Larry Rose, and all of the rest of them used to come down to the store. I started it in 1979 and 1980.

"And after the game, white kids went their way, black kids went their way. But this was the one place in town where kids would come together. They could all come and communicate together. They all would come over here and 'kick it.'

"Gene would bring white dudes into the black community and have a ball.

"As a little boy coming up, he thought he had it then. Growing up, I had a pawn shop. He would come back and say, 'Toney, I'm gonna do something in this town.' And he would bring guys like Bobby Humphrey here, come right here into town and talk to the little kids. Gene was one of the few guys who was on his way up, and we thought the world was Gene's. In the black community, he was one of the gifts but he didn't have anything to give but himself."

One telling incident seems to describe how tensions hadn't changed since the 1960's and have plowed through with the same attitudes in Etowah County to this very day. When the football team won that championship, the basketball team had made its way over to Tolbert's. The police saw some of the players outside of one of their cars and hanging out in front of the store.

To the Gadsden Police Department, that didn't look right...

Whites and blacks hanging out with one another outside a convenience store...???

Something had to be up and they were going to find out what it was... and put a stop to it right then and there...

They were about to put someone in the back of a patrol car- Tolbert doesn't remember who- with Gene and the Sansom players in plain view.

Tolbert had had enough...

He yelled at the cops that the kids were doing nothing wrong and he would call anyone and everyone he could think of to tell them about how the cops were "out of control."

"I could stand up to the police then," he admits. And you can still hear the disgust in his voice thirty years later.

"But not now...

"That was the last time I ever stood up to them and said that they didn't need any kind of permit, search warrant or anything like that. That was the last time I could stand up for young men because I knew what they were all about.

"That was the last time..."

Dan Jelks was a big part of his success. He was always with Gene, and was there to teach him not to forget where he came from. His dad kept them focused on not forgetting the relationships they were building, no matter how little or insignificant it seemed.

But, for a while anyway, football wasn't Gene's only sport. George Baker coached Gene in basketball and track. Baker also saw the potential that Ragland saw on the football field in the winter and spring.

"I met him in junior high school- seventh grade. He was an athlete, and I knew right off he had potential. It was amazing, and being his basketball and track coach, I helped him speed-wise with football- he was a special athlete... and he was exciting.

"He had the whole town buzzing. Everybody was proud of him and his achievements. I got the chance to watch for home games in the fall, and he was a tremendous athlete. He always had determination. When the spring came around, I coached him in track, and we had a 400M relay team. He was the fastest, and carried the anchor leg for the team."

Baker's relay team went to the state competition and finished second with Jelks running last. Gene also ran the 200 meters for Emma Sansom High School and that confidence Ragland saw was also witnessed first-hand by Coach Baker. But Gene wanted to work on his sprints- putting a close to a brief time playing basketball.

Baker does have one regret, however, about the time they shared on the track... that time they finished second at state...

"If I had done it again, I wouldn't have had him running anchor that day at state," Baker admits. In the second leg, they gained on us- this team out of Mobile. They got off to start good, but in the second leg he had to make up and in the third and fourth it was close at the finish. That second leg hurt me... but we had been running it that way. The baton pass was good, but for some reason, the guy didn't run his normal leg. We picked it up on the 3rd, and really pushed it on the anchor leg- we were a half-step short from winning it."

And who says coaches pains for losing get eased over time...???
30 years later and Coach Baker is still thinking about a close loss...

So, Gene leaves Sansom with a state title- and, as it turns out, the only title ever in school history. The 1980's were a decade at the school with all the star power that people remember and a decade where the team finished 52 games over .500. The decisions were to come as to where the stars would go to school. Weygand went on to a successful career at Auburn while Rose and Jelks ended up at Alabama.

A melancholy move to Gross, for sure...

"I would have liked to have seen him go to Auburn. I knew where he had to go and be happy. Looking back, I think he would have gone to Auburn and had a better time. I never tried to influence him in any way. These coaches are going to give you everything good about these places. You never hear the bad or normal things, but you have to be prepared for the bad. When I got back in to coaching, Etowah County High kids got sent over to me. Some started as freshmen in college, three started at Alabama as freshmen, one at Auburn as a freshman, and they played for me at that time. They were good athletes, and Gene was one of them.

"As far as I know Gene, he was a great kid."

"But that's all I knew...

"My senior year, I became the number one running back in the state- there was me and Bobby Humphrey out of Birmingham, but I was finally on my way. Nothing was going to distract me. However, there were people who supported me. I had my life made..."

"It all started in '83, I believe in my junior year. I was getting great reviews. The spin was that I was- the number one running back in the state if not the country. Bobby Humphrey was number two and Murray Hill was number three. Little did I know from Bobby Humphrey from Birmingham and Hill from Tuscumbia, I knew it was big with my home ec teacher coming to the school and people are coming to scout me.

"I stayed grounded and my mom kept us in church. I never knew anything about exposure in the next level besides high school. Once it hit me I enjoyed the feeling, but I stayed focused on improving my skills at becoming the number one RB in the state at that time. One of my most fond memories was I remember getting all these letters from Iowa, the schools in the Big 10, and the SEC... being a part of the Dixie Dozen 12.

"I never knew anything about all the national ratings, I was just a country boy from Gadsden. All it was was a couple of red lights, a skating rink and a church. So, it was a good feeling, but I didn't know I was about to tap into something big and get an education and live my dream- it was overwhelming- the whole school and community started supporting me- Caucasians, African-Americans, ministers would come by my family's house.

"Then I knew it was something big. God had given me a gift. People had always said that I was too little. I wouldn't be able to play at the next level. I never listened to the critics. My mom always said that you have to be patient, trust God, and you have to believe. She still says that to me today. I had critics all over the country, but I had great speed and quickness. They were also saying that 'he couldn't take that punishment at the next level.'

"My senior year, I became the number one running back in the state- there was me and Bobby Humphrey out of Birmingham. But I was finally on my way... nothing was going to distract me. However, there were people who supported me. I thought I had my life made...

"It was awesome and a great feeling knowing this could be my way out of poverty. It was very, very intriguing and exciting that the whole nation was recruiting me. It took away the sadness not knowing how I was going to go to school.

"It was a privilege and honor having Alabama and Auburn chasing after me. You only have so many scholarships and Alabama and Auburn are two of the most powerful universities in both overall athletics and football programs in the country. I didn't know the magnitude of what I really had at that time. It was one of the most gratifying, awesome feelings that a young person at the age of 16 or 17 could have having two of the major universities chasing after you to sign a letter of intent with their school.

"I was honored they were thinking of me...

"I think that a lot of my family went to Alabama, and some of my closest dear mother's friends went to the university. I remember my mother said to me at the press conference when I signed my letter of intent, she said, 'You make your own decision.'

"I remember Bo Jackson showing me around and he was straight and honest that you make your own decision. I still have the utmost respect for him to this day. Even though I know that I even out-rushed the Heisman in that historical game when I was in Tuscaloosa... He was a senior and I was a freshman and didn't know I was going to be facing him.

"Alabama showed me more things that I wanted to major in. I wanted to major in communications. Both schools are state-of-the-art and elite. No two schools in one state can say that.

"I felt more at home with Alabama than at Auburn, I didn't get all that much attention from Auburn after our state championship game my senior year. I didn't feel we had a connection- Pat Dye and me. I felt a distance between us. With Coach Ray Perkins, he called me more and visited me more when he could- due to the NCAA visiting rules as far as the times when you could visit.

So I knew that I wore 34 in high school. I was the leading rusher in high school and I couldn't wear 34 at Auburn. I knew they weren't going to let me wear 34 if I even thought about going to Auburn...

You know...??? Bo Jackson...??? Bo knows...???

"Auburn didn't want him," Jerry Pullen admits. "They had Brent Fullwood and Bo Jackson. The guy they really wanted was Larry Rose. But when Gene decided to go to Alabama, it made it more pleasurable for me."

Donald Harris also admits that when Gene chose Alabama over Auburn, it hurt him because he is a Tigers fan...

"I wanted him to go there, but you go where you've got to go. They gave him a scholarship. Just like Auburn did with Carnell Williams. So he had to go. Carnell went from Etowah to Auburn to the pros.

"Gene put us on the map. We are just a little, small hick town. But we're where Emma Sansom had the army cross."

And then, as a point of fact, Harris wonders aloud why the statue commemorating the defense of the town is on the Coosa River since "everyone" knows the Confederates crossed at Black Creek...

"He made me proud because I'm from the west side of Gadsden, a lot of people liked Gene."

Gene Jelks- the guy who wasn't the troublemaker... the "A" and "B" student who was educated and smart. The motivation to get out of Gadsden was to hide from molestation, and to be the first to go to school.

And it looked like he was getting out...

Gene's focus was to get some money and take care of his family. He grew up poor. So poor, as a matter of fact, that he says he couldn't afford the p, the double-o, or the r if you spotted him the letters to spell the word.

He would wear second-hand clothes, but it was cool. He wore them, but around the holidays, his parents used their own hard-earned dollars and would buy the Jelks kids new clothes.

He came from, in his mind, a great family. He had a dad who defended him, and as his son got better and better in his sport, he would say "Doris, leave that boy alone."

Dan Jelks was a warm man, protective of his family whose fabric came down to church, being poor, having love, having plenty to eat, and providing as best Dan and Doris could.

They even let him discover Church's Chicken. "But now that I'm older... that grease...???

"Get me a salad..."

Emma Sansom High Today- aka Emma Sansom Middle School

Chapter 3:

IT'S A BIG BUSINESS

The business of college football recruiting hasn't changed that much in the South...

It's still about big names, big money backers, and big dreams for all the kids who come from small towns to make their names in the cathedrals of Saturdays from August to December. Gene Jelks' road to Tuscaloosa from Gadsden had shades of most of what we know today as one of the four seasons of the calendar. It's not summer, fall, winter, and spring when it comes to college football in the South.

It's Football, Spring Football, Recruiting, and National Signing Day- and, yes, the capital letters are intentional.

It's that big a deal... and it's a big-time business...

For Gene, it meant getting phone calls from stars of Crimson Tide past- and the National Football League's past and present. For Gene, it was a chance to not look back and take those first steps in the goals he set for himself at Emma Sansom... the chance to pursue his dreams as a Miami Dolphin, being a pro football player, and being Gadsden's flag bearer for all of those thoughts in his head.

As he gets ready for the next stage of his life, the sound of the phone ringing in his house became a constant reminder of just how sought after he was for schools around the country...

Freshman year...

"One Sunday afternoon, my cousin Gene was over at the house," Gene remembers. "I get a call around six-ish. My cousin says, 'Telephone!' I didn't know about calls and recruiting and saying,

'Hi' to everyone who calls the house. He said that Ozzie Newsome was on the phone.

"I said 'You're lyin'!' So I got the phone and I said hello. The voice on the other end said," as Gene's voice goes very bass-like, 'This is Oz-zie New-some.'

"And I hung the phone up...

"He calls back... you know, I'm just a country boy. And I said, 'This is a joke.' There's nothing to do here in Gadsden... not to that magnitude... trying to make ends meet. We don't know these legends. I saw them on a black and white TV, where we had a wire plows and we adjusted the antenna with a hanger."

And it wasn't the only time Gene had a run-in with Alabama legends...

All he had to do was stay by the phone...

"The next week, I think my cousin was over again, it was another Sunday afternoon... I don't know what it is about Sunday. The telephone rings again. I said hello..." and this time it was an unmistakable, Pennsylvania-Tuscaloosa drawl- if there is such a thing...

"Joe Na-math... Howyadoin', Gene Jelks...?"

"I said, 'Fine.' I said, 'This is not Joe Namath.' He started giggling.

"And I hung the phone up on him, too..."

Gene's cousin, Reggie Adams, was with him for the recruiting trip to Tuscaloosa and got to meet Namath in person. It was one of those surreal moments in an 18-year-old's life, but Alabama wanted him and Gene hung up the phone on two Hall of Fame athletes. He knew the art of recruiting was the real thing to get him to run the football for the Crimson Tide. He also made a point where he didn't hang up on anyone else in the process. He was getting calls from guys who were made famous by pantyhose commercials just as much as they did by their football chops. Gene connected with those Alabama alums and they would, eventually, become mentors.

But once Gene signed on the line that was dotted and his time in Tuscaloosa was secured, it was time to get acquainted with his new roommate and Lower Gym...

Their first introduction to life as an Alabama football player and seeing if they were worthy of being a part of The Brotherhood...

"I first met Gene at a game he was playing," then-Alabama coach Ray Perkins says. "He had just returned a punt for a touchdown and I told the other coach that I was there with that I didn't need to see anymore. He was impressive."

When Perkins sat down with Gene and his mother, he was impressed with the family and the student-athlete he was trying to recruit. But he told Gene that he was also going to recruit Murry Hill and Bobby Humphrey at the same time. Perkins told all three the same thing- that if they were afraid of competition then they might not want to sign with the University of Alabama.

"He was eager to play football with the University of Alabama," Perkins continues. "A lot of kids have dreams to play football at Alabama and they, probably, still do to this day. Football in the state is pretty crazy. It is WAY, WAY, WAY up there. And I kind of like it that way. I always did. Even for me when I was in the eighth and ninth grade in school, I liked what I saw in Alabama football."

As did Gene...

He was a little small for running back. But Perkins came in himself on the small side at 170 pounds. Perkins was impressed with Gene's speed. By the coach's admission, Gene had more speed than a lot of the running backs in the country coming out of high school for the 1985 season.

"Speed kills," Perkins says, "and you can't coach that."

Kermit Kendrick is now an attorney with Burr and Forman, LLC in Birmingham and was another incoming freshman when they met for the first time. They reported early in the summer of 1985, and since they were the only two incoming freshmen at the time, they decided that they would be roommates. They got to know each other quickly and bonded pretty well.

At that point, the only students on campus at the University of Alabama were in summer school.

An interim session had just ended. Kermit and his parents decided it would be an idea to come in early and get acclimated to the college life.

"I think I came in on a Sunday," Kendrick remembers, "and Gene came on a Wednesday. We had big dreams. I remember vividly talking about the game against UGA and all we wanted to do was make sure we were on the plane going over to Athens.

"When we came in as freshmen, Alabama was coming off its first losing season in decades. The 1984 Crimson Tide was 5-6. Coach Perkins was determined to turn things around. He did a great job recruiting. The 1985 recruiting class included superstars like Gene, Bobby Humphrey, Greg Gilbert, Derrick Thomas, Howard Cross, Larry Rose, Anthony Smith, Al Bell, and several other great athletes.

"We had a great class. Twelve true freshmen started at some point in the 1985 season. We bonded with the older guys in a different way. They helped us get used to three-a-days, and we felt like we helped them go from a 5-6 team to 9-2-1 team."

But Gene entered his first summer in Tuscaloosa with a bit of a chip on his shoulder...

While what he accomplished was a rare feat, going from Emma Sansom to the University of Alabama, there still was the sense of wild-eyed wonder. It doesn't get any better than coming to play for one of the premier football programs in the country. He thought that this move was destined and a gift – given the talent he had developed. He still had to earn his place all over again in an entirely different setting, but as an incoming freshman there was one number Gene had in mind as his first goal on campus...

"I'm a no-name and haven't made a name for myself in the SEC," Gene says. "Coach Perkins never lied to me. If I can't wear #34 for the team (Ricky Thomas a linebacker was wearing it at the time), I don't know how it came to me, but I asked to wear number 22."

Whoops...

"Coach Perkins said to me that the number has been retired. I didn't know who the great Johnny Musso was at the time... I had to research him. The 'Italian Stallion...???' Whoa... I was completely blown away with what I found out.

"I knew, then, that I wouldn't get #22. I know Coach Perkins is a man of integrity and a Christian man and that he would never lie to me. I also asked him if I came in a freshman, would I get the chance to start...? He said that if I come in and work hard, I guarantee I will evaluate it with my staff. I'll give you an honest look. I remember and he didn't lie to me, he said, 'If I make that happen. That number is retired.' He never said a word. He said, 'We'll see.'"

As with most teenagers, Gene didn't like the idea of changing his number. It was good luck for him- and athletes have their rituals and superstitions. He would have to form a new identity. He would still be the same open, gregarious person on the field and off. But he would have to change numbers. And for an athlete... any athlete... to have to change a uniform number, it's like changing your whole routine.

You're changing your most basic form of identity and identification. You're having to tell everyone around you and everyone used to seeing you that you'll still be the same "Samson from Sansom" as it were...

You'll just look different.

It's like wearing your favorite pair of tennis shoes. You don't want to wear a new pair of tennis shoes when someone picks a pair up for you at the store. You want to wear the pair that's broken in and comfortable.

But Johnny Musso ended up being Gene's first homework assignment because of the possibility of a new number...

"I don't know if I'm going to wear #22 because of Johnny Musso," Gene admits. "I had to do research on him. I don't know who he is or where he lives. I didn't know anything about this guy from Chicago. I didn't know anything about an 'Italian Stallion.' So, I'm still a little hesitant if I'm gonna get #22 or not gonna get #22. My understanding with retired numbers is that it's done. I'm trying to fill the shoes of all these guys- Bart Starr, Richard Todd, Ray Perkins. The list just goes on and on- Sylvester Croom- all these legendary names...

"I have all these other running backs I had to compete with and I only weighed 155 pounds- and I still wanted to wear #22."

"Let me tell you something about Coach Perkins," Jerry Pullen says with conviction, "he always prides himself on giving people chances. I think his era in Tuscaloosa was misunderstood in a lot of ways the same way people may look differently about how he helped build the New York Giants."

Perkins gave Gene a chance and it also happened with someone who would, eventually, be his receptionist. He would go to the same fast food restaurant on his way to work and saw one woman working there that he recruited for his office. There was nothing to gain there, personally, Pullen reinforces that's just the kind of man Ray Perkins is.

Even if it came to number distribution. But you had to go through one other gentleman to do it.

Coach Bear Bryant's equipment manager was a carryover to the late 1980's- a man everyone called "Mister Meadows..."

Willie Meadows was the man in charge of every piece of equipment that was in Crimson color in Tuscaloosa. His status is of such a point of legend locally that, in this modern era of social media and remembrance, he has his own Facebook fan page that's active 15-plus years after his passing.

He gave advice on marriage: "Don't try to wear it out, it's like the World's Fair ... it gets bigger and better every year!"

Tide player Doug Faust tells a story before a game when he asked Mr. Meadows if he had been assigned a number: "Don't worry, we're not going to let you go out there without one."

He gave Greg Gilbert pink jocks and socks his freshman year on the team because he stayed in the training room so much. And he told an incoming student manager the first things he was going to do was cut his "goddamn" hair and "goddamn" beard because Coach Bryant didn't allow any "goddamn hippies" around here...

Meadows was the first line of the Tide defense, whether anyone admitted it or not... and Gene found out about that first hand...

"I didn't know what number I was going to get. I forgot about the whole thing," and, maybe for Gene, it wasn't a bad thing. "We get to the football facility. And I'm thinking Tuscaloosa is already the hottest place on earth.

Mister Meadows yelled "JELKS!" and it got Gene's attention... and his answer...

"I was a little, itty bitty country boy... scared to death... and he threw my jersey at me."

The pass was incomplete and it didn't sit well with Mister Meadows.

"Pick it up!" Meadows yelled...

"Yessir..."

"Whaddya waiting on...? And get the hell outta here!"

"I said 'Ohmigod,' and what have I gotten myself into...???

"And I picked it up and it was #22. I got chills I said, 'Wow.' That's a man of his word. Now, all I have to do is concentrate on learning the plays and have to wait for my opportunity to be a starter. Coach Perkins never persuaded me. He said, 'I'll put you in a position to give an opportunity.' Our first spring practice was with guys like Mike Shula, Freddie Robinson, Cornelius Bennett, and Wes Neighbors.

"Here I am watching these guys on TV and now I'm in a crimson uniform. It doesn't get any better than that...

"I'm just a country boy looking around with my mouth open, looking around, and coach says, 'C'mon, son, we got practice! This is not high school. This is the big league!' I can always take that to my grave.

God was making my dream coming true. It was amazing. It doesn't get any better than that. And still with my mouth open, I was staring and the coaches are getting on you at another level.

"Coaches are screaming and hollering at you... I haven't heard anything like this. Coach Gross put a lot of hard things on me. But at the next level, it's consistent. It's like a tune-up on your car. It's with you every day. The whole two-and-a-half hours, or three hours, two-a-days, and all the wear and tear on your body... it's all there. And it's still there to this day."

Gene still has those echoes of Mister Meadows and Coach Perkins in his head today. He was first put on the scout team and had to learn the pro-set offense from scratch. He had only heard about quarterback Mike Shula. The lifelong Miami Dolphins fan knew about Coach Shula- the NFL legend. Now, Gene was lining up on the same sideline with his son.

And Gene was rubbing off on his new teammates...

"My junior year, Gene was coming in for his freshman trip," running back Chris Goode says.

"With recruits, you hear about them and you want to go take a look at them. There was this small running back, but he has a lot of good stats and a great athlete. The first thing you remember is that you don't forget him, because he's a talker. He talked even more back then.

"Gene knew about all of the running backs coming in and you could see that he had a lot of confidence. Gene thought he was just as good. He was a real nice guy. He was just one of those guys that everybody liked."

"Gene was there after my redshirt freshman year," punter Chris Mohr remembers. "He had a good personality. He was outgoing and funny... people always told us that 'he went in a boy and left a man.' He was a quick running back and along with Bobby Humphrey and Kerry Goode before he had to have knee surgery."

"He was tiny. He was a little cat... a little tiny guy," linebacker Cornelius Bennett remembers. "The first thing that was different...? Bobby was a bigger version of Gene. He was a little Mercury Morris-type guy, or a Joe Washington. Those little fleas that people called them back in the day. He was tough, though. He came in and proved that as a freshman.

"Gene had the upper hand in competition between him and Bobby their first year on campus. When you're established like I was at the time, it's tough coming in as a true freshman. He got that by playing. As a leader on the team, I didn't allow guys to become big-head superstar-kind of guys. Gene fed into it and bought in to it. It helped him and I helped him through it, too.

"Coming in as true freshman, the notoriety you gain...??? Still... this is just after coach Bryant had passed away. Not a lot of freshman started under him. And then you have a true freshman coming in. It was unique and you try to keep him grounded."

"I knew who he was in high school," quarterback David Smith admitted since he played at a high school in the Gadsden area-Litchfield High School. "I knew who he was and I was there when he got there in 1985. I had red shirted the year before, but I didn't know him too much until the time when he got there with Bobby Humphrey.

"He was extremely talented and had very good instincts about football when he started as a running back, and he just could make things happen when he was out there. It made things a lot easier for me, or whoever was playing quarterback, that could turn and hand the ball off to somebody to run the ball.

When he and Bobby Humphrey were there, it was like we had never seen anyone do something like this before. Guys that could run as fast as they could, make the kinds of cuts they could make, and catch and do everything.

"I was very impressed with Gene and his ability when he got to campus. He got along with everybody and everybody got along with him. He didn't say a lot that first year, but he was an exceptional athlete.

"He had a little bit of everything and it showed during that season and in his first two years with Alabama. It was nice to have people with their ability to hand the ball off to..."

"Every Tuesday, we went over to Tuscaloosa to do the weekly interviews," then-Birmingham television sports anchor Gil Tyree says. "When he came in as a freshman, he was always accessible. He had a chance to do interviews with the local media. And at that time, Coach Perkins didn't allow freshmen to do interviews because of the maturation process and all that. Gene found a way to get interviewed for postgame situations since he played regularly. You saw a great personality. You saw someone who was genuine and could represent the University of Alabama as someone who was very articulate, smart, and liked to be in front of the camera."

"Gene was always full of life, was excited about being there at school, and a pleasure to be around," Kerry Goode recalls. "He was as a running back my sophomore season. For me, he and Bobby came in at the same time, and I knew eventually one of them would be the number one back- with what they were doing on the field- and both would put up a heck of a fight. But with both of them being rookies, I didn't put much stock into it the first year they were there.

"With Coach Perkins coming in, the way he was, if you could get the job done. He was gonna play you.

"Gene did everything. I never really saw any of the coaches get on him. He did everything he was supposed to do."

Not without the competition Gene knew would be a part of his time on the Crimson Tide offense...

Bobby Humphrey came in from Birmingham-Glenn High School and was thought to have a little more size and durability than Gene, but both would have to watch from the sidelines in the season opener against Georgia. Mike Shula would help bring the Tide 71 yards in five plays for the game-winning touchdown finding Al Bell from 17 yards out with 15 seconds left for the 20-16 win at Sanford Stadium.

But not without some hair-pulling moments... Torrie Webster blocked a Chris Mohr punt and Calvin Ruff fell on the ball in the end zone to give the Bulldogs the 16-13 lead with only 50 seconds remaining in the game.

"At UGA, they block a punt at the end and score," Kermit Kendrick recalls. "I remember the team not panicking, Shula not panicking, and instead of focusing on what happened, we had the chance to do something special and we did."

And it was the start of something special...

"I'm prouder of this victory than any other victory I've ever been associated in as a player or a coach," Coach Perkins said after the game. "This victory is what the doctor ordered for our football team. It really gave us a confidence in the arm."

Humphrey would get reps in the win against Texas A&M (30 yards) and both Bobby and Gene would get carries in the blowout win over Cincinnati. Humphrey had 106 yards and a score while Gene had 31 yards and a score. Bobby also had a pass reception for a score. And Bobby became the first freshman to record back-to-back 100 yard games with the 106 versus Cincinnati and 127 versus Vanderbilt the following week in a 40-20 win. Gene added to his touchdown totals with another one in the third quarter.

A loss to Penn State and wins against Tennessee and one at Memphis against the Tigers put the Tide at 5-2 heading into the Mississippi State game. A hamstring pull put Bobby on the sidelines nursing the injury- forcing limited carries- and gave Gene a chance to shine...

The win against the Bulldogs wasn't all that much in doubt with the Tide leading 31-6 at the break, but Gene would become the first Alabama player ever to have both a 100-yard rushing and 100-yard receiving game with 168 yards on 18 carries and catching 3 balls for another 120 yards in the 44-28 win to put the team at 6-2, 3-1 in the SEC.

"Gene Jelks had a great game," Coach Perkins admitted post-game. "During warmups, I had a feeling he would. Bobby Humphrey didn't play much due to a hamstring pull and Gene came through like I knew he would." The 288 yards of total offense gave Gene the offensive player of the game honors.

Gene would be the leading rusher in the 14-14 tie at LSU- 33 of his 91 coming on a first quarter touchdown run and he would put the Southern Miss win out of reach with a 4-yard TD run with under eight minutes to go in regulation for the 24-13 win on Senior Day.

"Legion Field is stuck... it is the most partisan example of football fever you could ever hope to see..."

For the uninitiated, the "Iron Bowl" is pure hatred... and ABC Sports was there for the 50th renewal of the Alabama-Auburn game November 30, 1985 at Legion Field with Keith Jackson and Frank Broyles calling it for a national audience. Tim Brant patrolled the sidelines, but Jackson's introduction under the video of all the colors, pageantry, and noise was a solid recognition of the life around him.

"Allegedly, it's split down the middle. Auburn folks think they still feel like the visitor when they come here. But... the tickets are supposedly split and they're both in good form today because you haven't been able to hear anything here for an hour..."

Alabama fans make a point to rub their nose in Auburn fans faces over the number of National Championships they've won over the years.

Auburn will make a point to remind Alabama that their claims by former Sports Information Director Wayne Atcheson of just, magically, adding six national titles into the folklore of the program don't sit well with much of the nation- much less those who live and die on the Plains.

Alabama will talk about all their All-Americans, and Auburn will remind everyone about their Heisman Trophy winners.

Bear Bryant said nothing mattered more than beating that "cow college down the road..."- even beating Notre Dame ten times- and didn't think Auburn took the sport seriously after calling over one morning at 6 a.m. only to have no one pick up the phone.

Pat Dye, at his first press conference, was asked how long it would take for him to beat Alabama.

He said: "60 minutes."

The week leading up to the 1986 game, Alabama Head Coach Ray Perkins allegedly made a comment that the game didn't mean as much to Dye because he didn't play at Auburn or Alabama.

After the game, Auburn QB Jeff Burger relays: **"When the coaches met at midfield, I saw Coach Dye get in Perkins' face. He told Perkins to look up at the scoreboard, and said, 'You wanna know what this game means to me? Look up at that scoreboard, big guy!'"**

It's "Punt, Bama, Punt," "Bo Over The Top," "Wrongway Bo," "Lawyer Tillman Reverse," Auburn's version of "The Kick," a home and home that "would never happen" until it actually did, "Bye-Bye Bo," "The Cam-back," tornadoes that happened a mile away and no one would leave the stadium...

And then there's Updyke...

Not just the one day a year the game is played- regardless of location past or present-but the other 364 days that people are exposed to it does that hatred and disregard for the other exist... could be on campus, on the phone, on the street, in the mall, in the bathroom... it doesn't matter...

It's always a part of the fabric of the state and will never go away... and, for the '85 season, it was Gene's coming-out party that would lead to Version 1 of "The Kick" by the time the game was over:

Russ Carreker' first-carry lick aside, quoting Kendrick again: "That's when Gene went off! The week of the Iron bowl- that week in practice, it was one of those things where you could see 'There you go.' It's one of those things where you look at him and you could see that he could play. You think to yourself that, hey, it'll be hard to move him out."

On the morning of the game, Gene had one of "those" run-ins with Auburn fans that both sides can tell you happen fairly regularly...

Like "365 days-a-year" regularly...

Gene was the standard nervous an 18-year-old would be in these situations. He was on his way to the team breakfast when a young Auburn fan, maybe 6-years-old, ran into him in the hotel lobby. The young man informed Gene that game day was also Bo Jackson's birthday.

"I said, 'Really?' Well, I am going to ruin his birthday today. I am going to outrush Bo Jackson! "Roll Tide!"

Early in the fourth quarter, Alabama was backed up to their own 10-yard line on a 3rd down and 4. Mike Shula handed off to Gene on an Auburn blitz. He found a hole on the near side, turned the corner, and almost broke it for the score.

Tom Powell saved the touchdown after a gain of 39 yards, but at the end of the run, as Jackson called it:

"Everybody in Gadsden... jump up and applaud! He's only a freshman, but he's the leading ground -gainer in the ballgame- 119 yards..."

"Gene could get around the corner when you saw no hope in it," lineman 'Hoss' Johnson says. "Gene just nipped the guy a little bit and he took care of the rest. It makes us linemen look good and you appreciated that.

"If you made the block it was definitely a plus for you!"

That running back named Jackson, that helped lead Jelks around campus when he visited the Plains, scored from the one to give Auburn a 17-16 lead with 7:03 to play. But the lead lasted 66 seconds as Gene responded with a run of his own on a 1st and 10...

"Here comes Jelks up the middle... pops it big... it's a foot-race to the corner...he's on his way... Powell's got a shot at him... closing ground...

"Touchdown!!! No flags..."

Broyles came in from behind with his analysis...

"Keith, there's no substitute for speed. Remember when Ray Perkins told us before the Georgia game... the speed that this young

man has is something special. He had an extra gear- something most backs don't have... that acceleration through the line and another gear to outrun the Auburn secondary.

Then, Broyles broke the play down on the replay as Gene put on the "after-burner..."

Once again, the great runners cut back because most of the Auburn defense was coming over in this direction. When he once cuts back, there was not an Auburn player over in that direction. Powell tries to get over there, but he couldn't do it.

"You've got to understand Gene a little bit," Kendrick says. "He's really proud of the 74-yard run. The game was back and forth. We needed somebody to make a play. I still watch the play back. I don't watch the kick. I just watch Gene drop it down into 5th gear watch him go down the sidelines. He was gone!

"He outran everybody. And then, Frank Broyles said 'Gone!' It's one of my favorite Alabama plays in history. And we knew when he broke it back, and if the linebacker or defensive back didn't get him, he was gone. All he needed was a half a step."

"I remember the long runs he had against Auburn," Kerry Goode agrees. "It was a breakout game and when he would hit second or third gear, he was gone."

"In the huddle it was loud," Johnson recalls. "We started moving the ball and Mike Shula called 'R-Toss 28.' But in the huddle Shula says, 'Let's go down on the first sound.' If you watch the play, we got in our stance and he says, 'Go!' or 'Blue!' We came off the ball and you notice Auburn's defense was still standing. They were moving on the line of scrimmage. They weren't fully set. They suspected something was going on when we went down quick.

"Gene cuts back to the left and, thankfully, I cut the defensive guy's legs when Gene was running that way. We all ran down to meet him in the endzone. There were a lot of great plays in that game, and that one was one of the greatest."

With less than 40 seconds left, Mike Shula would bring the Tide down the field. But he had to clear a 3rd and-18 obstacle first- from their own 12-yard line.

Guard David Gilmer returned to the huddle, as the story goes, and was really confident: "We've been in worse spots! We're going to score right here!"

Center Wes Neighbors thought he was crazy when asked about the play years later: "I'm thinking, 'David, you're wrong but I'm not going to argue with you.'"

Shula's third-down pass to Gene gained 14 yards, leaving Bama with a critical 4th-and-4 from the 26 with 29 ticks left.

"Mike's leadership on that drive was outstanding," Gene said after the game when he was asked about it. "There was no panic. We knew what we could do, because we'd been there before."

Rocky Felker called for a reverse from the press box. Pat Dye's defense keyed Gene- who handed off to Al Bell. Bell ran for 20 yards and a first down at the 46 with the help of a Shula block.

"An awesome block," Neighbors recalled. "Hit him right in the mouth."

Shula then found Greg Richardson on a crossing route, and a 19-yard gain before getting out of bounds at the Auburn 35, stopping the clock with six seconds left.

Van Tiffin's 52-yard field goal at the gun gave Alabama the 25-23 win.

Gene was given SEC Player of the Week honors and Sports Illustrated Player of the Week honors for his 192 yards rushing in the Iron Bowl- on only 18 carries- and it seemed his place was assured.

"It was one of the greatest games I've ever been associated with," Coach Perkins said afterwards.

"All year long, I've said this group of men has been special to work with. I'm just honored to be a part of this team and this game."

Gene would follow that performance up with Most Valuable Offensive Player of the Game performance in the Aloha Bowl win over Cal, 24-3.

"It's a very, very exciting and humbling emotional feeling to know you're on top in the SEC," Gene admits. "Bobby Humphrey was by my side. Murry Hill was by my side. I felt underrated. Tim Brando said I was underrated, but I never let the critics bother me.

"Because they always said I was too little, I was continuing to train, and eat right, so I can have a great future. I had to compete every day and it wasn't easy. The other running backs on campus might be a little faster or run a little harder, but I never gave up on myself. I love both of them to this day. We're good friends. Being number one and tapping into it on a high level on the field and off the field was what mattered."

1985 Alabama Season

9/2/1985	@ Georgia	W 20-16	
9/14/1985	Texas A&M	W 23-10	@Birmingham,AL
9/21/1985	Cincinnati	W 45-10	
9/28/1985	@ Vanderbilt	W 40-20	
10/12/1985	@ Penn State	L 17-19	
10/19/1985	Tennessee	L 14-16	@Birmingham,AL
10/26/1985	@ Memphis	W 28-9	
11/2/1985	Mississippi State	W 44-28	
11/9/1985	@ Louisiana State	T 14-14	
11/16/1985	Southern Mississippi	W 24-13	
11/30/1985	@ Auburn	W 25-23	Iron Bowl
12/28/1985	@ Southern California	W 24-3	Aloha Bow

1985 SEC Football Standings

	Conf	Perc	All	Perc	PF	PA	Home	Away
Florida	5-1	.833	9-1-1	.864	286	162	5-0-1	4-1
Tennessee	5-1	.833	9-1-2	.833	325	140	6-0-2	3-1
Alabama	4-1-1	.750	9-2-1	.792	318	181	4-1	5-1-1
LSU	4-1-1	.750	9-2-1	.792	227	134	4-2-1	5-0
Georgia	3-2-1	.583	7-3-2	.667	297	171	5-2-1	2-1-1
Auburn	3-3	.500	8-4	.667	344	208	6-2	2-2
Ole Miss	2-4	.333	4-6-1	.409	210	276	2-3	2-3-1
Vanderbilt	1-4-1	.250	3-7-1	.318	166	308	2-3-1	1-4
Kentucky	1-5	.167	5-6	.455	194	211	5-2	0-4
Mississippi St	0-6	.000	5-6	.455	257	288	4-2	1-4

Chapter 4:

WHERE CHAMPIONS ARE MADE

But... and there's a big "but" as a part of being an immediate contributor as a freshman. There's always a distance there between the underclassmen and the upperclassmen. Something is always going to put you apart, something that you haven't been through that the other guy has.

Even though you're there every day...

Even though you're contributing on game day and...

Even though you're winning games when the games are over...

But there's one place where you're tested, sorted, and eventually united...

Lower Gym...

Kermit Kendrick

"That's what they talk about the whole time you're there," Kermit Kendrick says...

And the laughter starts... he can laugh about it now...

"There are all those private winks and smiles while you're there: 'I wonder how he'll take it down there in the lower gym.' And so finally you go to the bowl game, and you come back and that's what faces you...

"I'll never forget the first time. You go down there on Tuesdays and Thursdays. You go down the steps, and it's dark. And you go to the room and they've got the heat cranked up to 95 degrees. They've got the four garbage cans in the corner, and from that point on it's just...

"To borrow a phrase from the streets... "It's on!

There's monkey rolling, bear crawling, suicides, crunches, anything and everything for about an hour.

And then they take you up to the concourse at Coleman Coliseum. You have to complete a run in a set time. And if you go through all that and you don't make the time, you have to come back at 5:30 the next morning. If you're leaning over tired, you have got to go back and do it all over again.

"I'm proud that I went through it, but it was not fun...

"I'll tell you what... after we finished, you're officially part of the group- you have proven yourself and have made it through something tough. When a guy like Cornelius Bennett pats you on the back and says, 'Good job,' you've gone through something special.

"You have to understand... we had some truly great football players there at that time- Cornelius Bennett, Larry Roberts, John Hand, Curt Jarvis, Freddie Robinson.

"When these guys put their arms around you... that meant something.

"Ray Perkins was the coach when we got there. Coach Perkins said we're going to win three games because of what we do in the lower gym. We believed we were special because of what we were doing in the lower gym.

Chris Mohr

"I almost quit after the first lower gym. Alabama had lost to Vanderbilt the year before, in 1984, and we finished 5-6. When Coach Perkins and strength and conditioning Coach Al Miller came in, we didn't know what to expect.

"I was in the second group that afternoon and a guy named Brett Nance came in after 20 minutes raising hell and tore up the shower heads. It was one of the most grueling things I've ever done. You would throw up just to rest.

"They would pick people to do '21's'- could be push-ups or sit-ups. You'd get to seven or eight and one of the coaches would say, 'Oh, Mohr's feet hit the ground.' And you'd have to start over. We'd do monkey rolls and shuttles, and then we'd go into the gym and run steps from the floor to the top. You'd have to have a foot on each one and hop while you're running to the top. I did my last set and Coach Miller said I missed a step. And there was no way I missed a step.

"I'd call my high school coach and all he'd tell me was to get some sleep because you'd have to do it again tomorrow. You got better at it and they weeded people out. We had Tuesday and Thursday groups, where on Monday and Wednesday nights, we'd have what we called 'Mourner's Row.' And from the six a.m. group, we'd always find out what they did- to mentally prepare you for what we were about to do.

"One day they said we were going to play basketball, and we were really excited about that. But then, they'd tell us that we couldn't dribble and it was all passing.

"You always remember the near-death experiences you have..."

Chris Goode

"It was one of those things everybody knew about it. Guys who were there before you tell about it. It was hard to imagine. Some fall over to the side at the trashcans. You're telling yourself: 'I can make it through this. It's not that hard.' It's sit-ups and crunches and you had guys falling over to the side without even running at the beginning. When you were through it, you knew this was the kind of guy who was dedicated and could go through it. It was the kind of guy you knew you could be with because this lower gym is really hard.

"We would have guys, four garbage cans- one in each corner. Many of the guys would throw up. It was so hot and it was non-stop, you never thought it would be so much work.

"Someone's legs would touch the ground and we'd hear... 'Whoops, we're starting over.' And the older guys are going: 'We don't need this.' They were just not used to it. You could have been a real good athlete and in really good shape and they wouldn't make it.

"Whatever drill you're doing... they were like 'Well, you just gave me a free one.' Sometimes all you could do is look at the guy. You knew it would happen with some people. And you would be in a group with some guy who would never make it. You're trying to figure out another time of day to come and do lower gym.

"You're looking around and you're going: 'He's not going to make it and you don't want to be in that group.'

"Once you had guys going through that type of training and you're giving the guys who struggle motivation telling them that they can do it. You give them a little push and you tell them 'Good job, Good job.' And you all know what they've been through.

"You come out and go, 'I'd go to war with this guy.' And basically, that's what it is. From your training to game time, you're going to war. You're doing the things you're doing and he's doing the things he's doing to make it a team and make that play to make it all work.

"It was a process for them. They came in and high school is totally different than college. They had to work and they saw that. A lot of times, people say 'Oh, they are there because of this or that.' But they had to work for it. Sometimes it just comes down to having that opportunity and getting that play to get in."

Kerry Goode

"They put you in a position where you are in groups- one fail... all fail. If one guy gets tired and he wants to stop by the trashcan, that means everybody stops by the trashcan and you start over. You had to uplift your brother and keep them motivated. For young guys coming in, you would hear stories, but you couldn't really... you didn't know what to expect until you got in there. And when you got in there, everything you were told was true.

"My only thing was for me, at that time, I was speed running and all that. Weight lifting, I thought, was going to be my biggest challenge and I thought they weren't going to give anything to me that I couldn't do. But I was wrong. I remember once getting on the squat rack, and I would go down, and I would keep going down all the way to the floor. But as far as the running and all that, I always said that there will be others who will quit long before I do. Because when they do, it'll be my chance to rest. So I never really concerned myself with the conditioning part of it.

"You never really would know what was in store for you, but they would keep changing it up. It could be jump rope, sit-ups, push-ups, but it was a complete mind game the whole time. They would turn the heat up, and you could be in that lower gym and they'll turn the heat up full blast. It's the winter and they turn the heat on, but you've got bodies running around in that gym and you don't need any heat.

"As soon as everybody goes in, they would lock the door behind you. You hear the sound of that door and it goes, "Ssssskkk." And you're thinking: 'What is going on in here....?' Everyone gets all stretched and loose. And then you hear "DOWN!" and you start your sit-ups.

"Then, you hear "UP!" and you have to hold it. And by the time you get to 15 or 20, someone in there is going all the way to the floor. So-and-so hit the floor and we would have to start over. Eventually, one of the upperclassmen would get ticked off and he would grab one of the younger guys and go,

'Listen... if you can't do it, just hold your arms, lock them out and don't do anything else.' They will accept that...

"But you do not fail!

"They wanted to put you in a situation where in the off-season would be more strenuous than anything you would face on the field. So, when you're on the field you've been through much worse than anything going on on Saturdays.

"Everybody was having fun on Saturday, because during the week you're asking yourself if you really want to play football."

David Smith

"Lower gym was an off season workout that started after we came back from Christmas break- from January until spring training started. It was a workout a couple of days a week. The heaters were cranked up and it was made to be as difficult a workout as they could possibly make it. Everybody had to finish. If one person didn't finish, we all didn't finish.

"There were a lot of tough times down there and sweat and other things down there. It also was a good time of team bonding as we were all going through the same thing. We all went through it together. It was extremely difficult physical and mental workouts while we were down there.

“And if you ever thought you needed to use the bucket, you used the bucket. You never went over there and didn’t use the bucket. You know what I mean? You didn’t want to go over there and get caught. I guess from the coaches down there, you were taking a break and it wasn’t allowed. We had mat drills, running drills, ‘21’, and all the different things. They were all extremely difficult and very challenging.

“You just got used to doing all of them. When people finished the first one, there were people who were already dreading the next one that was two days away. And that’s all they could talk about. I always liked going to the earliest one possible and get it over with-early in the morning. My last two years, I went as the early morning crew to get it over with.

“When you went later in the day, all you could do was worry about it and build up a lot of anxiety. I think it’s similar to what they do down there now in the Fourth Quarter program- I don’t even know what they do down there these days. I guess it’s very similar to that...

“You go through all of this with the guys you’re playing with- and you’ll be going up against the guys who are going to be tired in the fourth quarter because you know the ones who have been through Lower Gym are with you on the field together and you trust them. And it was building a lot of toughness and you could see just how far you could push yourself.

“You always found out that you could do just a little bit more than you thought you could, and people who haven’t been through that with you... it’s hard to grasp that.

“You’re completely exhausted and you have to do a little bit more. And you find you can do a little bit more. It drives you to be a little bit better every time.”

Kevin Turner

“I tried to block it out of my memory, but it definitely had that effect of making you a little bit better each time.

“It would be 5:30 or 6 a.m, down there under the Coliseum, no windows, no nothing...

"And when I was there, Rich Wingo was the strength and conditioning coach my first 3 years there. He was on the '78 and '79 National Championship teams. Rich was a fanatic about lower gym. He would put the heater on down there with no ventilation, so it's about 90-something to 100 degrees and 100 percent humidity and you're down there for 50 minutes to an hour.

"Once you start, you don't stop for 50 minutes. They set up big trashcans in every corner of the room for people to run over and puke in.

"You had to keep going after that... in reality, for most guys... you hated the night before and getting up and walking over there. But the whole day afterwards, you feel like you accomplished something. It was something where most guys pushed themselves through it. It's like the old adage, you don't know how far you can go until you have to. They set up an environment where you feel like you have to...

"If one person leans over or takes a knee, you're not even supposed to bend over and catch your breath unless you're puking. If one person leans over, everyone stops and has to start over what you were doing that day. Up-downs, whatever it was...

"You didn't want to be that one person...

"It was tough. We're starting out in lines in the gym and what we thought was stretching or something like that. It wasn't stretching. It was a workout with stations in every corner.

"I swear they used to have a contest to see who gets the most people to throw up or quit."

Chapter 5:

TURNING A CORNER

Sports Illustrated called the 1986 Alabama season- "the toughest schedule in the nation." The team would get as high as Number Two in the country before the loss to the eventual national champion- Penn State.

The season would be dedicated to George Scruggs and Willie Ryles. Scruggs was killed in an automobile accident a week after the A-Day game and had earned the "Johnny Musso Most Improved Back" Award. Ryles had initially collapsed on a Monday practice during a nine-on-seven drill after receiving a "normal blow" to the head as the team prepared for the Kickoff Classic with Ohio State.

Coach Perkins also said Ryles had complained of headaches for days before the workout. But he had been checked out and cleared to practice by team doctors. Ryles would collapse into a coma on the way to a local hospital and would be operated on for the clot, but would never regain consciousness. He was thought of as being a possible starter at defensive tackle and the deaths could have done one of two things- splinter the squad or bring them together.

It seemed to do the latter...

"It`s helped us come closer as a team," defensive back Rickie Thomas told the New York Times the week of the game. "People have been saying that we have a lot of talent coming in this fall, but I felt something was missing. This helps us draw closer together."

They would get the win without Cornelius Bennett, who had to sit out because of a hamstring injury. Gene would be the leading rusher on the day, and Bobby Humphrey would be close behind. Year Two of the tandem would pick right up where it left off...

"The '86 season was a situation where it was a combination of Gene and Bobby Humphrey," Gil Tyree says. "They dominated everything. Gene was also on special teams and he would also rotate in terms of how they would run the football. He and Bobby shared that. You saw the speed, desire, talent, and the idea that they wanted to do more. And from that aspect it wasn't 1, 2. It wasn't 1, 1A. It was really 1.

"You could see Coach Perkins had a luxury in terms of using both backs."

Actually, it was more than that and everyone had to prove themselves all over again. It wasn't just Jelks and Humphrey. It was Doug Allen, David Casteal, Kerry Goode, and Bo Wright thrown into the mix.

Gene would have a 75-yard run as a part of his 116 yards and a score in the game 2 win over Vanderbilt. He would be a part of the three-headed monster in the 31-17 win over Southern Miss, but then the season came to a screeching halt for him as he nursed a groin pull coming out of the Vandy game.

"Coach Perkins did a great job of keeping us together," Kermit Kendrick admits. "Gene was a major contributor, especially in games one through three. We beat Chris Chandler in the bowl game. We had a great team that year."

The defense came up big in the Florida game and, the following week, the Tide knocked off Notre Dame for the first time in five tries. Humphrey was the leading rusher both weeks. Add to that the 37-0 shutout over Memphis and another 105 yards and Coach Perkins was set to ride Humphrey as his new number one back.

The next week, like the Auburn game the year before for Gene, was Bobby's time on the national stage- in front of Gene as the back-up healed enough to get back in the game. Tennessee's defense gave up 217 yards to Humphrey- the most ever against the Volunteers- in a 56-28 win. Humphrey scored three times. Gene scored once on 89 yards.

Gene missed most of his time in the Tennessee game with what was called a sprained knee- while trying to get past the groin injury. He watched Bobby Humphrey get those 217 yards, but wanted to fight to get back in the game- regardless of how healthy he was.

Gene, however, says the injury was lower on the body and hurt his ability that much more.

"It was an injury to my ankle," he says, "and that was the difference. You have to be healthy and stay healthy to be able to perform at that high a level. I struggled with a high ankle sprain, but Coach Perkins was a no-nonsense kind of guy. He wanted to win. I couldn't perform and coach went with the healthier back at the time and it was Bobby Humphrey."

"My Pony's weren't working that day," he admits. "I was planting and I cut in my low heels and tweaked my ankle. I usually wear high tops. I didn't have them tied up the way I should have. I was getting into the swing of things with practice. We always made sure we had our ankles taped, or you were penalized if you didn't.

"At least you can comply. I didn't that day and it cost me."

He would find out just how much pretty quickly...

Gene felt a jumble of emotions that most 19-year-olds feel staring at that bum ankle. It's just that he was feeling them in front of tens of thousands of people on Saturdays with hundreds of thousands more hanging on his every movement Sunday through Friday. Looking back, Gene was trying to figure out how to deal with his naïvete, the pressure, the anxiety that goes with it, the disappointment in himself and what disappointment was felt by others, and just being flat out upset at what went down.

All at the same time...

"That demon still haunts me to this day," he continues. "It was a lot for a 19-year-old kid to digest. Coming from a freshman season and having a high ankle sprain, it does something to you emotionally and you see these great, healthy running backs that you beat out on the field. It takes a lot to maintain your sanity. There's nothing you can do with your body- it was frustration. I never imagined that I wouldn't have injuries my sophomore year.

"I was expecting to go in healthy. It wasn't healing quickly enough and Coach Perkins was checking with the trainers. Once I found out it was a business, I started to come at peace with a lot of things at the age of 19. I thought it was all about me, And that I would still have a starting job. That high ankle sprain set me back and by then Bobby Humphrey started progressing with his opportunity and was a lot of success. And I was his back up. There's a lot of frustration.

"The lesson is that reality is reality. There's a time to cry, a time to laugh, and you gotta take the bitter with the sweet. Going in, you have faith and when your opportunity comes again you have to make the most of it. The body is made not to take punishment. You have to be willing to take highs with the lows. You have to stay focused, and have a good attitude about it. Don't make rash decisions because you get negative consequences. The main thing is to believe in yourself. Accidents happen and things happen for a reason."

And Gene was trying to find out that reason for a very long time...

Both were stifled in the loss to Penn State, but then the Tide took out their frustrations for losing the game against the Nittany Lions in a 38-3 drubbing of Mississippi State in Starkville.

Humphrey bested his 217 yard performance with a school record 284 in 30 carries and three scores. His season total cleared 1,000 yards on the season with 1,004. Gene would contribute with another 61 yards and a score. But the distance was widening between his starting reps and back-up time. Humphrey continued his 100-yard plus performance in the loss to LSU and win over Temple and if there were any thoughts by outsiders that the job wasn't Humphrey's by then, his 204-yard Iron Bowl performance in a 21-17 loss and 1,477 total yards made it his to lose. Another 159 yard and two TD game in the Sun Bowl win over Washington cemented it.

Gene had come back from his injury, was ready to compete for the remainder of 1986, but he thinks he didn't get a fair shot to get his job back.

"I had six, seven, or eight running backs to compete with and I still feel my due just didn't come," he says.

And if he didn't think he had gotten his just due when he was healthy, things would get worse than that when the off-season came...

There was a lot of change coming to the Capstone and that's where Gene thinks his problems really began.

1986 Alabama Football Season

8/27/1986	@ Ohio State	W 16-10	@East Rutherford, NJ
9/6/1986	Vanderbilt	W 42-10	
9/13/1986	Southern Mississippi	W 31-17	@ Birmingham, A
9/20/1986	@ Florida	W 21-7	
10/4/1986	Notre Dame	W 28-10	@ Birmingham, AL
10/11/1986	Memphis	W 37-0	
10/18/1986	@ Tennessee	W 56-28	
10/25/1986	Penn State	L 3-23	
11/1/1986	@ Mississippi State	W 38-3	
11/8/1986	Louisiana State	L 10-14	@ Birmingham, AL
11/15/1986	Temple	W 24-14	
11/29/1986	@ Auburn	L 17-21	Iron Bowl
12/25/1986	@ Washington	W 28-6	Sun Bowl

1986 SEC Football Standings

School	W	L	T	Pct	W	L	T	Pct	PPG	Opp PPG
Louisiana St	9	3	0	.750	5	1	0	.833	25.5	15.4
Auburn	10	2	0	.833	4	2	0	.667	32.9	10.2
Alabama	10	3	0	.769	4	2	0	.667	27.0	12.5
Mississippi	8	3	1	.708	4	2	0	.667	20.0	13.9
Georgia	8	4	0	.667	4	2	0	.667	25.8	19.4
Tennessee	7	5	0	.583	3	3	0	.500	24.4	20.8
Florida	6	5	0	.545	2	4	0	.333	20.3	15.7
Miss State	6	5	0	.545	2	4	0	.333	17.7	25.0
Kentucky	5	5	1	.500	2	4	0	.333	20.7	18.8
Vanderbilt	1	10	0	.091	0	6	0	.000	17.5	31.5

1987

On New Year's Day, 1987, Cecil Hurt of the Tuscaloosa News wrote a column for the New York Times newspaper chain. Hurt's commentary, "Alabama fans will not fondly remember the Ray Perkins era," was a stinging indictment on the way Perkins ran his program for a four-year record of 32-15-1. But he was 2-2 against Auburn, 1-3 against Tennessee, 1-2-1 against LSU, and 1-3 against Penn State. But Hurt got to what he thought was the bottom of the argument:

"Bryant ran the program like a benevolent, if sometimes stern, grandfather. Perkins, on the other hand, ran the program like the chief accountant of the Bank of America.

"If you were on his side, the inside, a player or an assistant coach, he treated you well, just like any good boss treats his employees. If you were on the outside, though, things were different. And the fans, for the most part, were outsiders."

Hurt acknowledged Perkins made a good business decision. But the players were stunned... Dwight Lowry of the News caught up with Gene that same day:

"Personally, it was a big shock. I wish him well and all, but it really comes as a total shock to all of us. I'm just having a lot of mixed emotions about it right now. I don't know how we'll respond to this."

Gene told Lowry that the team had their normal meetings with Perkins in the weeks previous, but he hadn't hinted at a job change.

"We had a meeting and he told us of the rumors which had been spreading. But he told us he wasn't going to leave us. Apparently, he's changed his mind, as we've heard this morning.

"He was like a father to us. We really tried to put out a lot for the man and tried to play hard for him. He was a friend and we knew what he was about. I think it will affect the players a great deal, but it will just be a challenge for us to overcome."

But in the next breath, Gene admitted Perkins was more than a friend and a father.

"He's a man that loves his players. He was a fair man and his door was always open any time.

"When you were around him he'd make your adrenaline start flowing. He's a special man, and he'll be missed tremendously."

Dude Hennessey, a former Alabama assistant coach, was the one who recruited Perkins for Alabama. "Petal, Mississippi," he said in an interview with Sports Illustrated's John Underwood in September 1983. "Population 8,000. I got him with a 98¢ steak."

From Underwood's piece:

Hennessey says when he went to Petal to see Perkins he couldn't pry him loose from his job at the Sinclair gas station. "I asked if I could take him to breakfast. He said, 'I've got to wash trucks.' I said, 'How about lunch?' 'No, got to pump gas.' 'Dinner?' 'I got

to finish washing the trucks.' When I finally signed him, I took him across the river to Hattiesburg for dinner. I had in mind a nice, big juicy $10 steak, one for each of us. But he ordered a 98¢ hamburger steak, with onions, and iced tea. Naturally, I had to eat what he ate."

And that was the kind of fabric that was being lost to all of the players Perkins brought in, had mentored through the end of the Bryant recruiting class, and was now leaving behind as he went to the National Football League.

"It might always be Bryant's field and Bryant's place on the bus. What's wrong with that, anyway? I'm not replacing him, remember, I'm following him. I couldn't be prouder."

Perkins said that in the same SI interview, but now it was Curry replacing the man who replaced the legend... and that's what most folks want to be...

Bill Curry was the teammate Ray Perkins went to for advice when his playing days stopped in 1974 after a season with the Los Angeles Rams- 10 years spent in the NFL overall.

And now it was Curry's show... and a lot of folks weren't happy about it...

Jere Longman wrote about the hiring by then-Alabama President Joab Thomas in September of 1987 for the Philadelphia Inquirer:

Lee Roy Jordan, a former star with Alabama and the Dallas Cowboys, fired the loudest broadside at Curry's hiring. "If we're trying to end the Bear Bryant era at Alabama, we've made a giant step toward doing it," Jordan said. "I think Bill Curry is a fine guy. I knew him when I played against him in professional football. But his record for winning doesn't match his integrity."

A venomous letter sent to Thomas by one fan stated that "if (Curry) wins the national championship for the next 10 years, he won't be acceptable because he comes from Georgia Tech."

And, of course, there were the death threats. An anonymous caller told Tuscaloosa police that he had sent two men to hunt down Curry and kill him. The call was traced to a phone booth in Northwest Alabama. The caller wasn't found...

"It gives you some sense of the insanity that exists at certain levels of intercollegiate sports," Thomas said when the threats were made on Curry.

"And then when Coach Curry came aboard, things started to change a little bit in terms of the philosophy and Gene's contributions," Gil Tyree says. "You saw Bobby Humphrey get more carries. You saw Bobby Humphrey get more interviews. He was more the face of Crimson Tide football."

And then, when you ask Gene today, about the early part of 1987, his story changes from what he told the newspaper reporters at the first of year- understandably so, because The Brotherhood is there to protect The Brotherhood and to protect the University of Alabama first and foremost. It doesn't matter what is said in most situations outside the locker room as long as it's close to the story.

What's said inside the locker room, stays inside the locker room...

"When Coach Perkins leaves... that was a tough pill to swallow. He told us in our conference football meeting that he was in talks with the owner of the Tampa Bay Bucs, Hugh Culverhouse, and we knew Coach Perkins was a great candidate. He was like a father figure who I trusted. He was about to leave me and I was uncertain on what my future held. I had an idea and I wasn't real happy about it. My teammates and I were all disappointed.

"We had one of the strongest recruiting classes in 1985 that year and for our mentor possibly to leave us, all those rumors that he was leaving us and he did... I was sad and lost. Coach Perkins is someone who I still look up to this day, being a kid I still needed more guidance than I did. I shut down and it turned out a lot of the decisions I made hurt a lot of people.

"I was naïve and it never entered my mind that it was more than being just about football. This is a billion dollar industry. And once I figured out it was a business, I had to train my mindset and it was like I walked into a Fortune 500 company and didn't know how to run it. I was disappointed when Coach Perkins left and that 19-year-old kid that he could always communicate with would miss that.

"I think it's important to have someone who has been through the pros and cons to get that kind of advice. I think it was one of those missing links that Coach Perkins wasn't there."

"It was painful that first day when Curry showed up," Gene admits.

There was the standard amount of anger, betrayal, and hurt because for Gene- and for a lot of players on the 1987 squad- it was like losing either a father figure or a father altogether. For Gene, it looks like both were the case- even as he would be named "Running Back of the Year" by the Atlanta Touchdown Club.

"My sophomore to senior years were miserable years for me on campus," he continues. "I didn't know who to turn to. Kerry Goode was there. And I'm thankful that he's still in my corner today. He tried to help guide me. But, once again, I learned it was a business. It was not pretty when I found out it was a business. It's not like high school where everyone in community comes to see you. Then, you go on to the college level and you're lucky if you get a touchdown a year. You have that elite a player on the college level. My whole mindset changed."

Other things would change, too... but not in the way Gene anticipated or expected. And it would be the kind of event that would have him heading for the woods all over again. But that procession would be in the form of life-changing events that would happen in stops and starts, but once they started... they didn't stop...

"After the coaching change, Coach Curry and I meet and I'm positive and optimistic that I get the chance to sit down and evaluate where I am. I got back healthy. I was 100% going into my junior year, and I know I had to split time with Bobby.

"It wasn't fair what Curry did to me. He called me into his office and he said to me at the time that it was for the benefit of the team. I know now it was a much different thing at play. He said, 'I'm going to move you to defensive back.' He lied. He said that we didn't have any defensive backs and just crushed me.

"You crushed me, Bill Curry...

"I said, coach what are you talking about...???

"There was no trouble that I had caused. It was college rules. I know you have to compete at a high level. I never had to look or looked at the guys I had to beat out...

"It was wrong!

"It was just wrong at the time, Bill Curry, and I think he knows it to this day.

"I forgave him, but I won't forget. You don't take. You don't do that for your own personal career.

And I know he used me for his own personal gain. But that was a long time ago.

"And he also gave me a story in the office at the time about persuasion- he said something about 'people your size...' and 'You'll be good as a defensive back in the NFL.'

"But all you have to do is look at Emmitt Smith and all the NFL running backs smaller than me.

"It was wrong for Coach Curry to do that at the time to a 19-year-old athlete. Yeah, I was angry at the time. I was very angry at him for the longest time, but I forgive him these days."

"He told me it was politics. He told me that at Georgia State. He met me in the parking lot. And he said, 'I'm sorry.'

From the Alex Scarborough piece on ESPN.com from March, 2012:

But Jelks wasn't smiling that day. Before long, he was distraught and weeping, telling a blindsided Curry how much pain he had caused him.

Listening to Jelks unload years worth (sic) of trauma at his feet, Curry began second-guessing his memory of the day he told Jelks to move to defense. Curry said he "humbly apologized" and attempted to make things right. The two parted on good terms, but Jelks admits he hasn't yet come to an understanding with Curry.

"I think Curry was oblivious to it," Scarborough says. "You make so many decisions as a coach and you do them all with the perspective of helping your team and helping a player. I don't think he knew Gene was so hurt by this.

"Football is a sport that is so fast and so powerful, when you get hit it's 'life-amplified' as Curry told me. With Gene, that one instance has been amplified so far out that it has overtaken his whole life and he hangs on to it. Remember, Coach Curry went through the same thing with Vince Lombardi and got over it. Gene was the same way decades later."

Scarborough knew bits and pieces of the story, but more about the betrayal than anything else before he started to write about it. Sadly, he says, the kind of player Gene was throughout his entire career was lost in all of the anger. It took him over a month to track Gene down and try to convince him that the reporting was going to be fair. Alex also had to make sure he could get through Gene's general uneasiness of telling his story.

"You could tell he is deeply conflicted about it," Scarborough says. "You can see his joy and the ups and downs as well. His eyes would drop at some points and you could tell he was deeply concerned. He had great things to say about Coach Curry, but he wouldn't let go of the discrepancies he had. Gene had a good career. But with what happened after...? Some of it he wants to pawn off, but at the end of the day he takes responsibility for it.

"He still sees himself as 'his life would be okay if he was still a running back.' He doesn't see his successes as a defensive back and as a pro. He thinks politics were in play that kept him from a multi-decade career in the NFL. But for one instance with a coach, it would all be okay for him."

From Gene's perspective the effort that Gene was putting in on a position he had not played since middle school wasn't clicking in a way it needed to for success at a high-end, SEC, national championship pedigree program in college football.

It just wasn't...

"First of all, I never backed down," Gene admits. "I was miserable on defense. John Mangam was a mentor of mine. He was my position coach and took me under his wing. You only had so many days in the spring to learn the position. I couldn't plant right correctly to accelerate. I was born to run. My goal was to win the Heisman and be the first person to win the Heisman at the University of Alabama. It never happened because there were some who had the power over others and whatever you said went. I know some had a motive because they started running Bobby Humphrey for the Heisman. I know then, I was pushed out, it was obvious.

"I believe it was people behind the scenes that I'll never know who they are. I know something was wrong when it was a quick decision. It was an open and shut case. I should have transferred and gone on and pushed and pursued my dream as a running back in the NFL. I knew that's what I was destined to run...

"And a lot of people to this day want to know 'why?'"

It's not an answer Gene has, but he has been asked about it over the last quarter-century. Alabama fans have had the same question, but there are no answers that can prove the decisions that were made back then and can be satisfactorily explained to this day.

But, whatever made the decision stick, it stuck... and Gene was different from that moment on.

"I was changed. I say it was politics. It was too obvious," Gene says. "I went into his office and I said: 'Coach, you're making a mistake.' He said, 'I have these two great backs.' He admitted it 19 years later. Walter Lewis told me to call him. I was still bitter and angry and I was bickering back and forth with Walter on the phone and I said 'I'll call him.' He said you need to get it out of your heart before you can move forward. That's the best thing he ever said to me.

"It was obvious that he forced me on defense and told me a lie at the time and told me that I'd be a great defensive back at my size.

"Frankly, I just wish that my performance on the field would have been a deciding factor and not just something like a lack of defensive backs who could play Crimson Tide football. Let God and me make that decision with my ability with a football as to whether or not I was good enough of a running back.

"All I wanted to do was compete on the field at running back- that was where I was best. And I could have given the program a tremendous running back for the last two years of my career.

"I remembered someone asking me if I could learn the plays when they moved me to defense. And I said to that person that they insulted my intelligence. Why don't you go to Coach Perkins who has a pro-set mind and the mind set of coach Bear Bryant...? But I loved my team and I loved my teammates. I still do to this day.

"I went back to Coach Curry and told him that I'll go and play the position of right corner until you can recruit a corner back for ten days. After ten days, I went back into his office. And I asked him again to put me back on offense and I would be the best running back the team would have. Again... he ignored me- and I knew then I was stuck playing defense. I accepted the role and went into the meeting with the defensive coordinator, and he said 'Welcome.' I didn't speak to anyone. I was bitter and I was angry. I was mad as hell. I was sitting there with Derrick Thomas and he helped me with a lot of emotions.

"Bill Curry had given me a new position that I had to learn on the fly. And, to be honest looking back on it now, I should have transferred."

25 years later, though, if you ask Gene about that part of his life, he is more than sorry as to how he acted then. He was a 19-year-old student-athlete who was just angry at everyone and everything.

Nothing could stop that anger and bitterness toward his coach at the time. He has never been mad at the fans and followers of the program and its activity 365 days a year. But one event on campus as a sophomore made #22 stew for the next two years.

But, Gene was more than willing to go "old school" if that meant he could still run the ball.

"I thought I could do both offense and defense. At that time, I felt like I could split time like Deion Sanders. I was willing to split time at running back and defensive back to help us out.

"Bill Curry was selfish.

"He admitted it to me later in life. He said 'I was selfish, Gene.' He said he didn't know that I was that sensitive and I had a right to listen to you.

"Coach Curry told me: 'Gene, I'm sorry. I had two great running backs and I was selfish. And I made that decision to move you.' So, that was confirmation. And then they ran Bobby Humphrey for the Heisman. That should have been me. I, just as easily, could have been the first Heisman Trophy winner for the Crimson Tide. I believe if I hadn't tweaked my ankle and if Coach Ray Perkins was still there, I would have won the Heisman. Plus, I would have been over 1,000 yards as a freshman.

"I know if he had put me back on offense to compete with the other backs, and I had stayed healthy, I could have continued to be that back that made Alabama fans proud in my freshman year. But I don't think I could have done anything to change anyone's mind, sadly. I don't think Coach Curry, or anyone else for that matter, had any intentions to do that."

It has taken Gene a long time to deal with what happened. But if you ask him how he feels now...???

"I'm at peace with it now...

"He had a right to listen to me. I knew back then what the move was, but I had no power. I was just willing to be what I am today. He made, what I think was, a bad decision to make such an impactful decision on my life- and he did that as a head coach. Frankly, I think it should be God's decision as to how someone's life should be. I accept now what Coach did and I forgive him. But you never forget something like that.

"But once he said it on the record, 'I had two great running backs.' I accept his apology. But, yes, it has taken a long time for me to get to this point in my life.

"What I couldn't control was the severity of the business side and that it doesn't care about your talent. I was saddened, hurt, and devastated.

"I felt stripped by Bill Curry. In 1986, you have all these dreams in a box and all of a sudden the one you know you were destined to have was being cut out by the coach that has the power. What do you do? You're powerless. I believe in my heart that it was a wicked move. Maybe today others go through wicked things. I came from a family of love and was sheltered from those things. And I went into the SEC as a student-athlete. You have no power. You have no control. I can't describe it. People can sabotage your dream and I never know it came from a coach. He didn't have to do me any favors to be a special teams captain.

"But it was a very hollow act at the time as I look back on it. While I was honored to be given that and represent my team that way, I always thought that my place was on offense. I felt out-of-sorts and pushed aside, but I still tried my hardest when I was out there- even if I was mad about what happened."

And for someone who is so entrenched in the traditions of University of Alabama football and wants to represent the school he loves so much, there's one other act that can't be changed.

"My fingerprints aren't enshrined at the university capstone," Gene says with a touch of sadness.

"Only the offense and defensive captains are there.

"And I'll say it again. I could not be more disappointed about what happened that day in Coach Curry's office. I think that was another event in my life that turned my time in one direction instead of another."

Gene's 1987 season started out fairly well, so the average fan who didn't know what was happening behind the scenes would not be able to sense all the turmoil going on behind the scenes. His first quarter interception of a Southern Miss pass was good enough for a 31-yard return. David Smith threw a 16-yard pass to Clay Whitehurst with 7:20 left in the quarter for the first points in a 38-6 romp over the Golden Eagles.

Coach Curry said the right things about his team after the game: "Today was a good start, but it was only a start."

The Tide would go on to beat Penn State, lose to Florida, beat Vanderbilt and Southwestern Louisiana, and lose to Memphis State before handling Tennessee in front of more than 75,000 at Legion Field. Gene would shine on special teams when he caught a Bob Garmon punt on the run and took it back for a 63-yard touchdown giving Alabama a 14-0 lead on their way to a 41-22 win. He received his first "Bama Pride" award for his performance on the day and would follow that up with another one as the Tide beat Mississippi State the next week 21-18.

Game nine of the year was in Death Valley against LSU and Gene was a key performer on defense, and in the fourth quarter, he picked off Tigers QB Tom Hodson as he was looking for his first completion of the night. Gene ran it back to the LSU 30-yard line. Four plays later, Bobby Humphrey, ran the ball in from 10 yards away for the decisive score in the 22-10 win.

But the rest of the season was a disaster by all standards for Crimson Tide fans- an embarrassing loss to Notre Dame 37-6 in South Bend, a 10-0 shutout loss in the Iron Bowl, and a 28-24 loss to Michigan in the Hall of Fame Bowl in Tampa gave everyone a bad taste after a promising start.

1987 Alabama Football Season

9/5/1987	Southern Mississippi	W 38-6	@ Birmingham, AL
9/12/1987	@ Penn State	W 24-13	
9/19/1987	Florida	L 14-23	@ Birmingham, AL
9/26/1987	@ Vanderbilt	W 30-23	
10/3/1987	Louisiana-Lafayette	W 38-10	@ Birmingham, AL
10/10/1987	@ Memphis	L 10-13	
10/17/1987	Tennessee	W 41-22	@ Birmingham, AL
10/31/1987	Mississippi State	W 21-18	@ Birmingham, AL
11/7/1987	@ Louisiana State	W 22-10	
11/14/1987	@ Notre Dame	L 6-37	
11/27/1987	@ Auburn	L 0-10	Iron Bowl
1/2/1988	@ Michigan	L 24-28	Hall of Fame Bowl

1987 SEC Football Standings

School	W	L	T	Pct	W	L	T	Pct	Own	OppPPG
Auburn	9	1	2	.833	5	0	1	.917	26.2	11.0
Louisiana St	10	1	1	.875	5	1	0	.833	30.4	15.3
Tennessee	10	2	1	.808	4	1	1	.750	32.5	18.9
Georgia	9	3	0	.750	4	2	0	.667	25.9	17.0
Alabama	7	5	0	.583	4	2	0	.667	22.3	17.8
Florida	6	6	0	.500	3	3	0	.500	24.9	14.8
Kentucky	5	6	0	.455	1	5	0	.167	23.5	17.0
Miss State	4	7	0	.364	1	5	0	.167	15.4	23.5
Vanderbilt	4	7	0	.364	1	5	0	.167	26.0	32.3
Mississippi	3	8	0	.273	1	5	0	.167	20.3	28.1

You wouldn't know that Gene had a "bad year" statistically. He was seventh on the team in tackles with 65- 2 behind Derrick Thomas. He was second on the team in interceptions with 4 and even broke up four passes. He was the team's main punt returner and was third in kickoff returns.

But as you ask Gene, he's not impressed with any of it and was still mad that he had to play defense at all. It was almost a year-long protest move that ended up with good statistics- a true testament to his ability that Gene didn't notice until years later.

"It was pure world class talent," he admits. "Give all the credit to God. I was going through the motions and still succeeding. I was miserable. I dreaded to be in practice. I didn't have a good attitude and I was on auto-pilot my junior year. In 2013, I can look back and smile and look at accomplishing things others couldn't do.

"I just don't take any credit."

His friends, whether on the team or not, were shocked by the move. It was, admittedly, weird for them to see him at defensive back since he had all the successes as a starting running back before the injury his sophomore year.

One of his closest friends on the team was Derrick Thomas. Gene even wrote his first letter to his girlfriend in their college dorm. There would be times when they went home together over breaks, and Gene always thought that they were of the same heart. Thomas was a lot bigger, of course, but they had the camaraderie of the big-guy and the little-guy joined to do the same job. Thomas may have always been late for the plane, and had a cluttered room (which was a pet peeve of Gene's), but they were like brothers.

And the 1987 season with all of its changes for Gene was something that even the "bigger-same aged brother" couldn't talk about with the other.

"DT looked at me, but he wouldn't speak on it," Gene admits. "I'm glad he didn't. I tuned everybody out, just laid back and try to get through it. I like writing. And if you compare it to writing, it was more like an 'I'll put the pen down' kind of thing. I just kept quiet, internal, and just dealt with it."

It was suggested by one of Gene's family members that he transfer. If you try to pin down his emotions, you could say he was some combination of numb, frustrated, angry, disappointed, and confused. Once again, all of these emotions are happening at the same time with a 20-year-old young man. And it seemed like too much for Gene to handle, even though it looked like he was handling it to the outside world. He thought about transferring to Clemson because he liked their offensive set. But he didn't follow his intuition and the advice he was getting.

And the question remains: What does he think would have happened if he had transferred...? Would his future been any different...?

Gene could have been stuck behind another group of talented running backs- regardless of where he would have transferred to in the Southeast. And it had to be in the Southeast so he could be close to his family. If he had been an 18-year-old all over again he might have been able to go to school in a Big-10 or Big-12 Conference school. But he was too vested by this point heading into his junior season. It had to be close or he had to stay.

And he chose the latter... he wanted the chance to outperform his competition and outdo any critics and criticisms. He had signed with, what Gene thought was, one of the best two schools in the country after being recruited by every school in the nation. That kind of attention builds anyone's confidence up, but his bed had been made.

"I should have transferred, but I was scared. I kept quiet. I didn't even discuss this with one person. In all fairness, I was miserable at defensive back at Alabama and I was going through the motions."

He had one more year of going through those motions, and his senior season started off well with a 96-yard kickoff return to start the third quarter in the 37-0 shutout of Temple. The next week with a 44-10 blowout of Vanderbilt, Gene had a 37-yard punt return for a score in the first quarter.

"It was Astroturf... concrete and a little carpet at Vanderbilt," Gene admits. "I think I was leading the nation in punt returns at the time. I, kind of, remember what happened. They had just punted. It was 4th down, and we had 'return right' on. I caught the ball on a high punt. I could make the decision to make a fair catch, go up the middle, call 'punt right,' or 'punt left.'

"I caught the punt at the 38 or 39 yard line. I would always set the defense up the way we practice. I could tell my secret today. I would always shift the punt team. I would call for a shift, run that way for two or three yards, and then come back quickly in the call so blockers could set up the return. I could get through little holes and I ran like I was running up the middle. We set up the right return and that gave my blockers a chance to set up the wall for the touchdown.

But on the next set of downs from scrimmage, Gene blew out his knee covering a Commodores wide receiver.

His season was over...

And, Bobby Humphrey's career would be over later in the same game. Early in the fourth quarter, he re-broke his left foot and was also done for those who followed them both in Tuscaloosa.

Two players, whose careers and actions were so linked together over a four year period, were done in the same game left to think about their futures- one seemingly secure, one more in question than before.

"Then, I get back on defense," Gene remembers. "The tight end for Vandy was 6-5, 250 pounds. On 3rd down, they were looking for mismatch. I knew I had a short field, and they couldn't run a quick out to the short side. I used the sideline as another defender like you're taught. He ran out of bounds. I read it right, backpedaled, pushed him out of bounds, jumped over him, and all my weight landed on my right knee. I heard something pop and snap like a rubber band. It was my ACL. And I knew it when the team doctors took a look at it. In five or ten minutes, the whole knee swelled up and they said the knee was totally and completely gone. They totally were going to have to reconstruct it. I just put my head down and started crying and I didn't know what my life was going to be like after that.

"Could the old injury have been a part of this one...? It's a possibility. Accidents are accidents. The only way that you survive is by staying healthy. Think about it...? Two of your running backs go down in the same game...? It's a devastating loss to both of us and the football program, and the fans.

"I cried. Bobby Humphrey and I both got hurt in the same game. It was a painful experience for both of us. I was bitter and disappointed with all the rehabs, the pain, the surgery... it goes on and on. You have to wear a brace for so many days and weeks of training after the operation.

"But I just stopped doing it...this is my third challenge."

The first thing Gene did was call his mother. He said that he wanted to come home. He talked to a student counselor on campus and found out he had enough hours banked to take a semester off. He went home and was in one of those fogs that very few know how to get out of with any idea of where you're going or what caused you to get there...

"I was empty... very empty. It was only by God's permission that I endured that. Family, friends, whoever, church people, all their prayers really helped me stay stable. I couldn't sleep. And I was in a lot of pain. I chose to get away for a while. My mom came and got me and got me away from campus, but the whole thing was a nightmare."

Gene admits now that what happened his senior season was something he could dwell on from that moment forward, so when he runs into another difficult experience he has a reference point on how to react and get around how no matter how bad the situation is-turning a negative into a positive...

But as a 22-year-old...??? He didn't have the mental capacity to wrap his head around what had happened and what was happening.

"It was scary," Gene admits, "and I was real uncertain. What am I going to do now...???

"It was a scary moment. And because I didn't rehab like I should, I just end up going home to be with my mom and be with my family. I just did not rehab the way I should have. I admit that as a man today. I take all that responsibility that I didn't rehab like I should have due to the trauma I went through. It's not an excuse. But if I could do one thing different, I would have rehabbed 100-percent. I would have called my mother, but not to take me home. That whole thing was a setback.

"At that time, I needed nourishment from my family. The coaches were going on 'next.' It's a business, there's no other way to put it. You had the top running back in the state coming out of high school and, after two years, you push him to defense. It's a business."

The hardest lesson for any young man to learn having to do with big-time college athletics...

And Gene learned it over and over his last two years on campus...

The 1988 season had to survive the "Hurricane Bowl" and the "Rumor Bowl" at the same time where interim university president, Dr. Roger Sayers, having to address the notion that Bill Curry's job was not secure at the same time Texas A&M had to address Jackie Sherrill's future. With all the injuries, all the chaos, all the distractions, and all the grinding, it took a Sun Bowl record-setting performance by David Smith to end the season with a win.

1988 Alabama Football Season

9/10/1988	@ Temple	W 37-0	
9/24/1988	Vanderbilt	W 44-10	
10/1/1988	@ Kentucky	W 31-27	
10/8/1988	Mississippi	L 12-22	
10/15/1988	@ Tennessee	W 28-20	
10/22/1988	Penn State	W 8-3	@ Birmingham, AL
10/29/1988	@ Mississippi State	W 53-34	
11/5/1988	Louisiana State	L 18-19	
11/12/1988	Louisiana-Lafayette	W 17-0	@ Birmingham, AL
11/25/1988	@ Auburn	L 10-15	Iron Bowl
12/1/1988	@ Texas A&M	W 30-10	
12/24/1988	@ Army	W 29-28	Sun Bowl

1988 SEC Football Standings

School	W	L	T	Pct	W	L	T	Pct	Own	OppPPG
Auburn	10	2	0	.833	6	1	0	.857	28.2	7.7
Louisiana St	8	4	0	.667	6	1	0	.857	20.8	17.0
Georgia	9	3	0	.750	5	2	0	.714	29.8	17.7
Alabama	9	3	0	.750	4	3	0	.571	26.4	15.7
Florida	7	5	0	.583	4	3	0	.571	22.3	15.4
Mississippi	5	6	0	.455	3	4	0	.429	20.1	20.3
Tennessee	5	6	0	.455	3	4	0	.429	19.3	26.0
Kentucky	5	6	0	.455	2	5	0	.286	19.7	18.9
Vanderbilt	3	8	0	.273	2	5	0	.286	18.4	25.2
Miss State	1	10	0	.091	0	7	0	.000	15.6	30.2

1989

Gene would return for a footnote to his career in the 1989 year-exclusively as a punt and kick returner in 8 games during the season.

He was involved in 39 plays for the season- averaging 6 yards per punt return and a little over 21 yards per kickoff return. The Tide would go 10-2 in, what would be, Bill Curry's last season in Tuscaloosa- losing to Miami in the Sugar Bowl 33-25.

On January 8, 1990, Curry would resign from his post and Gene would leave the Capstone at the same time.

Curry told Cecil Hurt and Andrew Carroll of the Tuscaloosa News that it was because of the "inordinate pressure being brought to bear on people I was sworn to serve" that was the reason for his departure. It wasn't money, but the pressure on his family, staff, and team which according to the coach "went hand-in-hand."

He wouldn't specify the "pressure," but admitted that "the controversy of my mere presence here caused great difficulty" for his team.

And that can never be in dispute...

1989 Alabama Football Season

9/16/1989	Memphis	W 35-7	@ Birmingham, AL
9/23/1989	Kentucky	W 15-3	
9/30/1989	@ Vanderbilt	W 20-14	
10/7/1989	@ Mississippi	W 62-27	@ Jackson, MS
10/14/1989	Louisiana-Lafayette	W 24-17	
10/21/1989	Tennessee	W 47-30	@ Birmingham, AL
10/28/1989	@ Penn State	W 17-16	
11/4/1989	Mississippi State	W 23-10	@ Birmingham, AL
11/11/1989	@ Louisiana State	W 32-16	
11/18/1989	Southern Mississippi	W 37-14	
12/2/1989	@ Auburn	L 20-30	Iron Bowl
1/1/1990	@ Miami (FL)	L 25-33	Sugar Bowl

1989 SEC Football Standings

School	W	L	T	Pct	W	L	T	Pct	Own	OppPPG
Tennessee	11	1	0	.917	6	1	0	.857	28.8	18.1
Alabama	10	2	0	.833	6	1	0	.857	29.8	18.1
Auburn	10	2	0	.833	6	1	0	.857	23.7	10.9
Mississippi	8	4	0	.667	4	3	0	.571	25.8	26.2
Florida	7	5	0	.583	4	3	0	.571	22.3	16.8
Georgia	6	6	0	.500	4	3	0	.571	20.9	16.5
Kentucky	6	5	0	.545	2	5	0	.286	19.3	20.0
LSU	4	7	0	.364	2	5	0	.286	26.8	22.9
Miss State	5	6	0	.455	1	6	0	.143	18.6	18.8
Vanderbilt	1	10	0	.091	0	7	0	.000	14.7	24.1

Chapter 6:

ON HIS OWN

Welcome to the pros...

"I went on with the Broncos, Charlie Waters was my position coach. I was competing with Atwater, Braxton, Henderson, and I get burned on a play. I just didn't know them. I learned that pro ball is a billion-dollar industry. I remember signing the contract and it didn't feel right. I was out of place. I would have liked to have been pushed to the NFL being a running back- not a defensive back or just a kick returner. All I know now is that I should have consulted with someone about transferring.

"I had the perfect world, I had it made. As a freshman, safe to say, I was one of the top running backs in the country. I had it made. No reservations. But I accept it today. Kids these days playing sports are going to have more mountains to climb and valleys to walk through. You don't expect the reality to set in after the difficult times. But, there's more bad than good to talk about where my life has gone.

"I was getting that second lesson about good and bad- this time as an athlete. I never did discuss things as an athlete with anyone. I was naive. After being molested, this was the second hardest lesson and I was afraid to go to my family all over again.

"Playing street ball on the street growing up and playing on the dirt in a pile... it was my world. All I was focused on was football.

"And we all see what happened..."

Bobby Humphrey was on that roster as a second-year player, too. He was that added dimension that the Broncos were lacking in past seasons that would eventually give them a shot at Super Bowl XXIV in 1989- a game that they would get blown out in by San Francisco 55-10.

But with return duties in Kevin Clark's hands as well, Gene's shot at the NFL was done even on a team that would finish the year 5-11 not making the playoffs.

He had been drafted in the first round of the CFL Draft by the Winnipeg Blue Bombers and Gene's impression at the time in an interview with Jimmy Smothers of the Gadsden Times newspaper that the future was bright:

"They want me as a running back," he told him at the time. "They already have punt and kickoff return men, already so that's out. I might play defensive back, but that would be my decision."

Gene also told Smothers that he knew that the change to defense was going to cost him a lot of money- and it did since he went undrafted. Gene said that scouts would ask "why didn't Bill Curry play him?"

His agent, at the time, told him not to go to the NFL Combine because, if he had a poor combine he wouldn't be drafted at all. So, his advice was not to go and his stock took that final hit.

Through it all, however, Gene told Smothers:

"...regardless of anything else, I will always support the University of Alabama. I love this school, always have, always will."

He would end up in the Canadian Football League for two seasons as a kick returner, mainly, in Winnipeg- against the initial plans- and the time up North soured him even further.

Chapter 7:
ONE MAN TO ANOTHER

It all started with a guy named Larry...

Or Gene thinks it was a guy named Larry.

That's what he remembers about the whirlwind of the next few years.

Larry visited him at the house where his mother, Doris, lived in as Gene was substitute teaching in Gadsden. He had also sold cars in Birmingham and worked at a sports memorabilia shop in town.

Larry's talk hit home for Gene. Larry presented a bunch of checks that Gadsden businessman Harold Simmons had written him while he was in school. Simmons was a Jimmy Dean distributor and hired Gene to do some work for him to pick up some cash.

In an interview with ESPN.com's Alex Scarborough in 2012, Jelks recounted what Larry told him and what would follow in Gene's mind:

"(Larry) said, 'I knew Alabama did you wrong. You were a great, elite running back, and I liked to watch you run.' He said, 'I'm not a fan, not of Auburn or Alabama; I'm a businessman.' He made that distinctly clear. I said, 'What is this about?' He said, 'They did you wrong, and you deserve revenge.'

"And all of the sudden, it clicked. That's when the light came on. That's when the evil side came on me. My mother said, 'Don't do it,' and my grandmother said to let it go and move on. I didn't. I made up in my mind."

From then on, Gene Jelks was ready to bring the whole house down with him- and it didn't matter who was a part of the damage. His anger, to tell you the truth, first popped up before the Sugar Bowl in what would be his last college football game.

Then-sports reporter and columnist for The Birmingham Post-Herald, Ray Melick, had seen Gene get mad in New Orleans the night before #2 played #7. Melick recounted how, in front of Keith McCants and fellow writer Paul Finebaum, Gene burst in ready to tell anyone willing to listen what was going on. He wanted to be interviewed. He wanted to go public and he wanted to "rip Curry to shreds."

In November of 1992, he did just that...

Gene Jelks said he was paid thousands of dollars by coaches and school boosters during his career. In an interview with the Atlanta Journal-Constitution's Mike Fish, Jelks said that: "I was bought and sold to the university."

From Fish:

He said money was funneled to him and his mother while he was still in high school to obligate him to play for the Crimson Tide. The NCAA, which prohibits such payments, has contacted Jelks' attorney about the allegations.

Jelks claims his mother, Doris, and then-Alabama assistant coach Jerry Pullen orchestrated his signing in 1985 when he was in high school. Everyone, naturally, denied this including his mother, Doris.

This was a very heated time off the field for Auburn and Alabama supporters. A year after Eric Ramsey revealed his secretly recorded tapes and allegations of illegal cash payments in his time at Auburn, Jelks has produced his own tapes alleging NCAA violations by Alabama. Jelks said he taped conversations with his former middle-school coach, Jerry Pullen, and others to document what he said went down. The payments included a $2,100 signing bonus after he enrolled at Alabama and money to help him make payments on a car.

From Melick's work:

"I feel like Gene feels he was done wrong," said Larry Rose, a four-year starter at Alabama who played high school ball with

Gene in Gadsden. "He was booted to defense when he should have been left at running back. They moved him to defense to push Bobby (Humphrey) for the Heisman and it crushed him.

"I feel sorry for Gene. And I'm worried about Gene.

"He's the one who will end up hurt from all of this."

Teammate Philip Brown agreed:

"From knowing Gene, he likes to be in the limelight," Brown said. "He's proud of himself. He always wanted to accomplish something. Maybe he... a lot of black ball players feel like we were exploited. We played and practiced a lot and got nothing to show for it.

"That's why, when you go down there, you have to realize that if worse comes to worse, you can get a degree. Nobody is being used, other than using yourself."

"If Gene was getting that kind of money, it would have been visible," Rose said. "He would not have been fighting and scratching to get by like everyone else was."

Brown again:

"Having been around him four years, going to bowl games with him, double-dating with him- there was never any money," Brown said. "I roomed with Cornelius Bennett, and if Cornelius wasn't getting money, surely Gene was not. And Cornelius wasn't."

PR/Safety John Cassimus:

"When everything was going well, Gene was the greatest guy in the world. He was everybody's friend. But he hurt his knee against Vanderbilt (as a sophomore) and he didn't rehab the leg. He didn't work hard. It was as if he expected the leg to get better by itself.

When he came back, Bobby Humphrey was doing well and Gene was moved to defensive back. He was very jealous of Bobby. He was bitter."

Coach Ray Perkins:

"This is a tragedy. It's going to hurt Gene Jelks more than he realizes. It's the same with that other guy at Auburn."

Harold Simmons, listed at one point as one of the ten most influential college football boosters in the 1980's and 1990's admitted he gave Jelks jobs, but he didn't do anything illegal.

"He is broke, grabbing straws," Simmons told the Journal-Constitution when the story broke. "He had some bad luck. He didn't make it in pro ball. Eric Ramsey hit, and that's the only limelight he sees."

He accused Alan Cohn of paying him $100 a week to wash trucks, and Gene said he would leave after only washing one truck.

"I don't know what the man is talking about," Cohn told the Journal-Constitution's Mike Fish after admitting he was "dumbfounded" by what Gene said. "He is mad at everybody connected with the University of Alabama."

Atlanta attorney Stan Kreimer- a UVA grad who got his law degree from the University of Georgia, was the son-in-law of Jack Swertferger (Auburn, Class of 1952). Jack and his wife Ann were season ticket holders and members of the Soaring Eagles Club at the time.

Kreimer would then become Gene's attorney...

Kreimer said publicly that he was referred to Gene by "a network of attorneys in Alabama." When asked initially, he refused to say how Jelks was getting paid or who was picking up Jelks' expenses. Gene was living in Atlanta at the time and odds were that no one was going to give Gene a job at any time in the near... or faraway... future.

Even Gene's father, Dan, spoke out: "It really disturbs me to hear something like that. I know we didn't get any money. If we did, we haven't seen it. What bothers me is why did Gene wait so long to talk? Why didn't we hear any of this years ago? Something is wrong with this."

Gene fired back at anyone willing to hear his side: "At this point, I'm 26 and I still have these guys trying to bribe me to keep me quiet. Giving me $100 here, or helping me out there, or telling me what a great job I'm doing. They feed me a bunch of lies. I'm tired of this. It's time to get on with my life, to take control. Any mistakes now, I have no one to blame...

"This is Gene Jelks' idea. Nobody came to me. This is not the Eric Ramsey story. The (Alabama) alumni, when I called them, they thought that this was a joke. They know Gene Jelks. All they did was buy me off all the time, buy me off to keep me quiet."

Gene also accused Alabama assistant Rockey Felker of paying him almost $600 for a Christmas present he would buy for his mother and another $600 for playoff wins his senior season at Emma Sansom. Felker had relocated to the University of Tulsa by 1992 and would not comment publicly short of one quote to the Associated Press:

"He called me out of the blue and made some accusations about me and illegal recruiting. I knew something was going on then."

Gene's mom had no idea what was going on... even as she and Jerry Pullen were named as the two people who were responsible for having Gene sign with Alabama. Gene said he had taped conversations with Pullen and other individuals who were involved in the exchange of money and goods.

In the conversation, according to the Atlanta Journal-Constitution, Pullen is heard saying:

"People don't know anything unless you tell them. You might have this call on tape for all I know. In other words, what you're saying is you should have gone somewhere for free. You shouldn't have been bought. That's what you're saying."

And, then, talk went to the Ford Escort:

Just after Christmas in 1992, Jelks was interviewed by the Journal-Constitution again. He said a Gadsden businessman co-signed a $13,000 loan during his senior season and that Simmons paid two ex-Crimson Tide players, Stacy Harrison and Clyde Goode, to be grand marshals in a 1991 Christmas parade in Altoona, Alabama- the home of Exchange Bank, the bank that executed the loan in the first place. Jelks told NCAA investigators that the money from the loan was used to purchase personal injury insurance.

He would appear on CNN and explain that the loan was for $9,000 and that he received the money from the loan during his junior season at Alabama. Gene would not repay the loan admitting that he was "struggling... These people were telling me what to do and how to do it."

Simmons and Goode would deny the payments, but Simmons would admit he asked Gene to "line up" players for the event.

Gene would make public six checks written by Simmons from June 12, 1989 to January of 1990 for a total of $1100 that he did get from Simmons. At least two of the checks were written during football season, which could have been considered an NCAA violation. Gene would also talk of the alumni handshakes that make college football famous for the wrong reason- telling CNN that after one game he wound up with $400 in hand after greeting powerful alums.

But Chris Goode did say when asked about the parade payments that Jelks defaulted on a car loan he cosigned for him in April 1990. The loan was almost $20,000.

The car in question...??? A Ford Escort...

But someone who saw Gene grow up in Gadsden and was very close to him stated the car came from a different source.

"When he graduated," Jackie McNutt says, "Doris said 'I need to find him a cheap car.' My cousin sells cars. He tells me, 'I have got one right now- a beige Escort.' I called Doris, told her it was a super clean car, only two years old, I will put right side on it, and my cousin asked if he can meet me in the bank downtown. He had never met Gene's mom before. And there she was when we showed up.

"I introduced him and his mom said 'Y'all go do your transaction,' and I'm going to work at Goodyear. Gene called me and said 'What about this car momma got me? What about this car momma got me?' I said, 'Your momma got the car for you as a graduation present so you could go back and forth from school and financed it down at the bank.' She bought it from my cousin. You don't believe me...? Ask him. That's what I told him!

"He was a stupid little kid doing something out of spite when he lashed out. When I heard it, I was in New Orleans, I would have gone through the TV and slapped him! I never stopped liking him, but I told him that when you find Jesus, you'll find me. When he was living under the bridge for three years later in life, I told him that if you would have called me I would have come and got you. But he was bitter with Bill Curry!

"Curry couldn't coach himself if there was one player out on the field. Coach Dye said once on the radio he never understood why he moved Gene. He had a Heisman trophy winner – every three times he touched the ball it was a TD, even back in high school."

Pullen and Jelks even got into a fight at McNutt's business in the neighboring town of Glencoe when Gene's life was spiraling out of control.

"Jerry calls me up and says I want to talk to Gene," McNutt continues. "I told them that I'll go to the back office so they can talk. 15 minutes later, they're holding each other, love-tapping, and I get in the middle and sling them both around. My door comes unglued. The outside panel slapped the frame.

Jackie still hasn't repaired the door to this day. But depending on who you ask, the tenor and tone of the meeting was different.

Alex Scarborough caught up with Pullen in 2012 who said:

"...it was Gene who called the meeting, looking for more money. Pullen said Jelks was getting boxed out by his Auburn backers, and wanted to meet with him to talk about the idea of turning them in-for a price.

Pullen left and Jelks never met with the NCAA after that."

Gene says that, in the Scarborough piece:

I said, 'Jerry Pullen, you owe me.' He said, 'I know.' I said, 'You've been riding me since junior high.' "He said, 'Please, don't say anything. Whatever you need, we'll work something out.' He was begging and pleading. I said, 'Coach, you don't understand.'"

That's when Jelks says Pullen got up and barreled across the room at him.

"He tried to tackle me, and I jumped back," Jelks said. "I said, 'What are you doing, Jerry?' He said, 'You're going to tell them!' We actually fought. We were in a tussle. He was so angry and mad."

"A week later, I get a phone call," Jackie continues. "Gene calls me. He wanted to know about the Escort.

"And I said to him, 'I told you once I told you a thousand times. Your momma bought the car from my cousin. She financed it at the bank for your graduation present. So you could come home back and forth to and from school. Don't ask me anymore, I'm tired of it. You want to ask someone, ask your momma. And, oh by the way, you can tell (Auburn mega-booster Bobby) Lowder and the attorney and everyone there in the back that if any of you print my name or say one word about me that I'm going to own everything they got and the University of Auburn. And the first thing I'm going to do is have a weenie roast and I'm gonna fry it."

Gene and Jackie's conversation ended right there.

"Gene told me years later that the lawyers said that day, 'Don't none of y'all mess with him!'"

Jackie would, then, get a phone call from the Atlanta Journal-Constitution shortly thereafter. The reporter wanted to ask questions about Gene:

"'Is this Mister Mac-nutt...?'

"I said 'Jackie would be fine.'

"I wanted to ask a few questions about Gene Jelks.

I told him, "Sir, if you print my name, I'm going to sue the AJC. I got nothing to do with it.

"Guess who I'm going to find first...?"

"You! Because I'm going to fire you! Do I make myself clear...?"

Gene had abandoned the Escort and was looking for another car to drive. McNutt knew of another car Gene could have of Jackie's- a little Geo that he drove back and forth to his shop. Jackie gave Gene the car to drive and Gene went and hocked it because he needed the cash. Jackie went after Gene over the phone:

"I started yelling at him going, 'Where's my car? Don't get me mad... Where's my car...???!!!' I called this guy up that you got it from. You got my car now go get my car, because all you did was just throw your money down a wild hog prairie! When this conversation is over, I'm coming to get my car, or I'm gonna see the sheriff. He and I are real good friends.

"Jackie sent Gene over there and told Gene that he 'better give him the car.' He got my car!"

Jackie once told Gene a story. His grandmother once told him to go get some milk. As it turned out that one time, he didn't go get any milk. He went and got tassels put on his shoes. Sufficed to say, he almost got beaten to death. Guess what...? The next time out when his grandmother asked him to get just the milk...???

He went and got the milk...

Jackie hoped that Gene would learn the same lesson... But it would take a very long time...

"There were Alabama alumni that wanted to kill him," Donald Harris admits. "I'm just telling you pointblank. Gene had to get a bodyguard to stay alive. He hired two bodyguards right out of Atlanta. One of them was about 6-4, weighed about 300 pounds. And the other guy was, like, 6-3 280. Yeah, they had death threats on the man. There were people who wanted to take him out and put his head in the ground. He had to get out of Alabama.

"I think he went to Atlanta, Georgia, and that's why I say I wish he had shut his mouth. They hurt him, so in his mind, they were going to hurt him back. He did no wrong. When they took him off offense and put him on defense, it messed up his career."

"When Gene first came on campus," 'Hoss' Johnson remembers, "we knew he was feisty, friendly, and fast. When he got the football, we were always thinking; 'Let's see what is going to happen!' Gene was a slasher and interesting to watch."

After the Denise LaSalle remake of the old Fats Domino tune, they would always say: "Don't mess with my 2-2!" mixing Gene's number on his back with the song of the time. But when Gene did what he did in going public, Johnson thought his actions violated The Brotherhood.

"It's a wound inside of the family. You wonder why he would do that. You want to find out what happened, what the specifics are, and you hate to see it happen. It, really, affected both schools in the state of Alabama. It really affected The Brotherhood because it looked like he has turned on you.

"It really upsets and grieves you and you want to know the whole story. Some players wanted to know the short version and didn't want to talk to him again. Others wanted to know how we could help him and wanted to go deeper and find out what really happened. I think that's the unique part if it now. Several of us wanted to help him out and help him succeed."

So, just how did the checks get into Gene's hands...???

According to a Gene Wojciechowski piece in the Los Angeles Times from August 3, 1995, it was a divorce proceeding:

"Harold Simmons and his wife, Carol filed for divorce. Business records and canceled checks were turned over to Ms. Simmons attorney, Steve Brunson–an Auburn booster and supporter. The

checks were written by Harold Simmons to Jelks between June 12, 1989 and January 6, 1990 and were cashed by Jelks.

"Brunson sent the checks to a Montgomery attorney, John Thrasher, who was a huge Auburn supporter. Brunson and Thrower in turn gave the checks to another Auburn booster, Atlanta attorney, Stan Kreimer. Kreimer, then sent copies to the Atlanta Constitution and was used as evidence in the Jelks allegations."

The last Simmons had seen of the checks, they were in the possession of either his ex-wife, Carol, or Gadsden attorney Steve Brunson.

Auburn supporter John Thrower said Stan Kreimer contacted him three times between November 2 and 5, by telephone, in person, and by fax in 1993, but Thrower claimed he had already destroyed the copies and refused to help Kreimer.

Simmons knew four people had access- himself, his ex-wife Carol, Brunson, and Eddie

Cunningham- the attorney who handled Carol Simmons' divorce two years after Brunson.

Simmons said when asked about their whereabouts:

"I had the checks. They were gotten from me by my ex-wife. She took them to Steve Brunson two years ago. From there, Steve Brunson held them two years. The attorney she hired had to get them from Steve Brunson. That was Eddie Cunningham. The checks were never in anybody's hands but us four people.

"Now, I know I didn't give them to Kreimer, I know she didn't give them to him. I know Eddie Cunningham didn't give them to him. So that only leaves one person."

A partner for the law firm of Simmons, Brunson, and McCain told the Birmingham Post-Herald when asked about the checks: "Certainly, he nor anybody in this office turned any kind of information over to anybody. We have no business records. We retained no business records.

Everyone has accused Brunson of this, but it didn't happen."

How did the copies get to Kreimer: "That is a concern of ours as well..."

Thrower says he got the checks through a "friend..." telling Mike Fish, then of the Journal-Constitution, that a dead Auburn fan gave them to him.

Thrower admits being approached by Kreimer... But... telling Fish...

"I will swear on a million Bibles I didn't give him or anyone copies of those checks."

"I was sitting in my office on Marietta Street," Fish recalls about his time at the AJC covering the Jelks story. "Some people called and said they had this guy, a former player, who had received money from boosters and that there are three or four people who want to meet with me. That night, I was going to drive down to a truck stop or fast a food restaurant near the Alabama border... at 10:00 at night. The whole thing sounded bizarre and crazy. I enlisted (fellow AJC writer) Jack Wilkinson with me to drive down there.

"I want to say there were three or four guys in a Cadillac, and they introduce themselves. We chatted for an hour or so. It was just bizarre. You couldn't recreate or imagine this thing if you tried. The license plate was covered in mud. It was a real Keystone Cops situation. We're sitting in the car, one guy is on the phone in the restaurant, and they're trying to give us copies of the documents. One person got clearance and they turned over copies of cancelled checks from my angle. Then, I was trying to track down folks, and eventually I got to talk to Jelks, Simmons, visit another small town, and started the process of histrionics. This whole story was at the heart of the Alabama-Auburn rivalry."

Ray Melick was covering the story for the Birmingham Post-Herald at the time:

"I had been covering the Auburn situation with Eric Ramsey. Auburn fans were upset and felt Alabama fans were behind the investigation despite Ramsey's tapes. It came out of Jelks allegations, and during the early days of the allegations nobody could find Gene. I was sitting in the Post-Herald offices, and a young lady calls and says that Gene feels he has been mistreated. Here's his phone number and he wants to talk to you.

"It was a Saturday, and he was a little surprised, and Gene wanted to know how I got his number. I told him I was a reporter and I didn't know where I was going with this. He told me a very elaborate story about Auburn boosters coming up to him and telling him that they would take care of him- pay him to get ready for another tryout for testimony against Pullen- telling how he was recruited and try to 'get to' Alabama.

"I remember writing a story on a Sunday, calling some of the people who had allegedly been taking care of Gene. I found the father-in-law of one of the attorneys and called explaining what I was doing. A few minutes later, I get a phone call from the man, then, confirming that I had Gene Jelks' number and he laughed it off. This exposed the rivalry to a certain extent and the extent fans would go to and pay Gene Jelks in a hotel room to get at Alabama.

"I think they were using Gene. I think that is unfortunate because there was a guy in Gene who needed to be helped out and have people take care of him. And it was an example of football fans who were trying to achieve a better end and weren't looking out for Gene's best interest.

"At the end of the day, there wasn't much evidence to back all that stuff up that Gene brought forward. Even in the NCAA investigation, they thought Gene's testimony wasn't all that reliable.

"He wasn't what got Alabama in trouble. But it opened up that door and put Alabama on probation.

"With the Jerry Pullen situation, there were so many fishy characters, lawyers violating attorney-client privilege, discrepancies, and revealing things they shouldn't have been revealed.

"This was one of the undersides of college fandom that was felt on for the next decade in the state of Alabama."

Simmons would eventually sue Thrower and Brunson for publicizing the checks in the first place.

And the game would go as far, on the surface, as having a Birmingham sports-talk show host saying on-air that Thrower and his associates paid Gene Jelks $170,000 to say his peace in public.

The Wojciechowski article would go on to say the promises for Gene to speak would come close to matching that figure:

There is documentation of bank records showing that Jelks' received close to $67,000 from an escrow account with Kreimer's law firm, with the promise of $200,000 when and if his allegations brought the Crimson Tide down. When the allegations began, a $30,000 slush fund was created by Pat Dye along with Wayne Hall to pay Jelks and to keep him talking to investigators at all cost.

The slush fund was even discussed in an interview that Auburn head coach Terry Bowden gave to Paul Davis in April of 2001 when Bowden found out he inherited a pay system for athletes and recruits that was orchestrated by mega-booster Bobby Lowder:

Bowden said the corruption extended to former head coach Pat Dye, and included $30,000 to Atlanta attorneys for Gene Jelks in order to sustain the former University of Alabama player while he leveled charges of wrongdoing in the Crimson Tide program.

Bowden said he learned of the major NCAA infractions within days of being named Auburn's head coach, but kept quiet while trying to clean up the program from within. "I broke the rules," Bowden said. "I told Wayne Hall to pay it off to the players we already had and it will never happen again. I was hiding a dirty secret."

Bowden said the payment of players can be traced to Lowder, who Bowden said is the unquestioned leader of the AU athletic department."

Nothing was done without Lowder knowing." Wayne Hall and Pat Dye paid $30,000 for lawyers in Atlanta to keep Gene Jelks talking.

When Gene's allegations didn't wash with the NCAA's investigation of the information he presented, what it did do was send them into the direction of defensive back Antonio Langham and his signature on a cocktail napkin the night after the Sugar Bowl. Langham signed with Darryl Dennis what Dennis claimed was a legally-binding document to represent him after his college days. Langham would play in all of the 1993 Alabama football games before being declared ineligible.

The program would be placed on three years' probation in August of 1995. The Crimson Tide was banned from participating in bowl games for a year, had its scholarship numbers cut over a two year period, and had to forfeit eight wins and a tie in which Langham played for Alabama in 1993.

But the battle wasn't over for Gene and Jerry Pullen... It was just beginning...

Chapter 8

PULLEN VS. JELKS

Jerry Pullen was a Graduate Assistant under Ray Perkins after spending some time with "Brother" Oliver's staff at Tennessee-Chattanooga. He worked hard and recruited hard by phone- the Gadsden connections helping immensely with Rockey Felker as the lead recruiter. Pullen could still go to games back home in Gadsden because his brother was playing. It was not considered any kind of NCAA violation. Pullen also brought in Al Bell from Coffeyville Junior College in Kansas and Darren Whitlock- five lettermen.

Over the phone...

Which meant Perkins put him on the road as soon as he could...

He cared about the kids he recruited and Gene was no different.

But Pullen had had enough and decided to sue Gene Jelks for defamation in a suburban Atlanta courtroom in 1994. One of Pullen's attorneys, Tom Cauthorn, said in court that he believed Gene had been paid to go public with his allegations. Cauthorn tried to get Gene's financial records entered as evidence in court, but Judge Warren wouldn't allow it. She rendered, in her verdict on that motion, that the Alabama newspapers that claimed he was "put up" to those allegations was "hearsay" and, therefore, inadmissible.

But the case went on... famous Alabama booster Logan Young even "loaned" $4,000 to help pay Pullen's legal fees.

Case Number 5922-8 in Superior Court: Jerry Pullen vs. Gene Jelks

The DeKalb County Courthouse- The home of Pullen vs. Jelks

Gene's mom, in January of 1994, would even give a deposition reversing her previous opinion of not knowing what was going on with her son's allegations when he went public in 1992.

The quote, initially, tied to Doris Jelks was: "What would I look like selling one of my kids?"

She would say in her deposition that it was Pullen who figured out the sale of the Ford Escort, knew how it was paid for, and delivered cash to her monthly to pay off the loan of the car.

Fish tracked down Doris and Dan Jelks and her response to him was quick before she hung up the phone:

"I don't have anything to say to you about that deposition. Really, it was supposed to be confidential in that room."

And, if you ask Doris Jelks today about it, her memory of that time twenty years ago is faint at best.

Stan Kreimer went on the offensive on January 27 to the Tuscaloosa News- even to the point of disclosing Gene's father, Dan, was there when the payments were made in a plain, white envelope:

"The main thing I would like to say is Mr. Pullen's attorneys have completely distorted the text of the audiotape and my client's deposition in order to show there is a contradiction (in Jelks's charges), and that is not so. There is no contradiction. My client's story has been consistent from the start."

But, in discussing the nature of the phone call where Gene recorded Pullen two years before, Gene first said he made the call from a pay phone, but later admitted the call was made from a phone in Frost's office.

Randy Edwards- one of Pullen's legal team members on the charges...

"It just didn't happen.

"We had mutual friends. Jerry was a graduate assistant after I left. My first few years in Seattle, I would come back in the off-season to campus and work out while my wife went to graduate school. So I knew him, but didn't know him that well. Some other guys that knew me better than he did knew that he coached. So when everything broke down I was talking to Wes Neighbors. He was telling me 'this is just a lie, we've got witnesses that can prove that they're putting him up to this. Can you talk to him?' I said sure...

"I talked to him, and we got involved in the case...

"We believed Jerry's story that it was completely made up and that he was being coached on how to make statements that didn't sound good on the tape recorder. One of our goals in discovery was to find out who was helping him, because one of our beliefs was that he was being financed by a group of people who wanted to have him come forward to make these allegations. That was one – what his story was and this alleged buying of the car took place, 2) Where did the car come from? Who bought it for him, and who made the payments? How did he decide to come forward, and show up in Atlanta of all places... Was he being paid for his story and who was paying him...?

"We never went to trial. The first step was that we had to find out the story about the car and when we got into that, it made absolutely no sense. It wasn't plausible. We talked to the guy who sold the car to Gene's mother and he denied that there were any shenanigans going on. We deposed Gene's mother. And her story was that every week or so, Jerry Pullen would drive to Gadsden and hand her an envelope full of cash, and when we pinned her down on it, it just wasn't plausible for Jerry to be doing what he was doing in Tuscaloosa and then being in Gadsden at 5:00. It was clearly not possible.

"We deposed her and Gene and we talked to the seller of the car. They deposed Jerry and that was, basically, it. The way it all shook down, they filed a motion for summary judgment. (That's where the party defending the case gets to discovery and- you say, 'Judge, here's the undisputed facts, and when you apply the law, and we win.')

"Their motion was based on the tape recording that Gene had made. Jerry had made some in-artful statements. Things like: 'What are you talking about? No one knows anything about that.' At 11:00 at night, they woke him out of a dead sleep. But the judge had ruled that he had admitted the truth of the allegations and in a defamation case, truth is an absolute defense. She said that since he had admitted the allegations during the phone conversations, we had no case. So she tossed it out.

"That was a year into the case. Jerry has been selling medical supplies and hasn't coached since. He had moved on with his life."

"At the time, Jerry was very upset- very bitter.

"It was sad to me that Gene would do this. That he would turn on his university and his friends and he turned on every friend he ever had at the university? It was disappointing that he would do that... he was very bitter about how his career played out at Alabama. He was moved to defensive back since we had another great running back. It didn't work out, and he blamed his disappointments on the other people.

"We never found out who was paying him. We heard rumors who was paying him. It's disgusting for people to have enough of a vendetta to and pay him to do this- to use money to bring down somebody else, it's disgusting instead of spending their money for good."

The end thought from Edwards in all of this...

"People need to step back and have a reality check it's just a football game- from that to Harvey Updyke."

Tommy Deas- Sports Editor, Tuscaloosa News

"I remember covering that thing! It was a hoot. Basically, we found out that Gene had been given, originally, $40,000 in the discovery filing. So, what you do is show up at the courthouse, pay for the copy fees at 5-cents a page, and you get the latest filing..."

"But coverage was deep and off the charts when the judge in the case, Linda Warren Hunter, signed off on a "gag order," but the legal proceedings got outsmarted for a while- even during the trial.

"It was another one of those 'player is on the payroll' stories- So, Stan Kreimer asked for a gag order and that the filings be sealed when they're made. If lawyer A filed a motion or discovery at 8 or 9 AM- whenever the courthouse opened on that day, it would go into the work flow in a basket and placed at the file at the end of the day.

"Once it was filed, you couldn't touch it because it had been protected or sealed. The people working the desk didn't know it was sealed. So, you might get a tip and drive in at 4 in the morning and get to Atlanta- get ready for a filing, more often than not, it could come from other side. We would go in, walk up to the clerk and say that 'We understand there was a filing in the case today, can we get a copy today?'

"They're dealing with hundreds of cases. And the judge was getting furious!

"She was going: 'Are you handing them copies of all this stuff...?' admonishing the lawyers in the courtroom. Lawyers can put their hand on the bible, because they have developed relationships and say they hadn't done anything. I would show up once or twice and there would be reporters from rival newspapers in the other line going after the same information. One time, we got tipped off- we even said to one another that there are hundreds of pages to sort through, why don't we just work separately, and split the cost of a hotel room. And when you can't do it in public, you go into a hotel room… That way, we had a workplace and hundreds and hundreds of pages spilt on a bed."

"One time I showed up, got in line, and one of the lawyers was at the head of the line. I'm three people behind, the lawyer walked out, and I asked for a copy of what he just filed. There was some subterfuge among reporters- even in the media work room. Some of our bosses were like, 'I don't want him to know we're going to Atlanta,' but we would be staying in same room doing the same thing...

"I was the one who got the $40,000 payout information out. It was big news over there. It hadn't been reported much, then that was reported and it was a big deal...

"I think the math came out to $39,000 and change that was documented. It was, definitely, something you could hang your hat on. I remember getting my calculator adding it all out- it was labeled for rent or something like that... no reporter had gotten it. Gene had made public comments before, and there were comments that allegedly caused the lawsuit. From there it became, 'Where's Gene Jelks?' We were looking for addresses, and people would say that he 'doesn't live there anymore.' He had never talked publicly during all that...

"The important thing, to me, is that he's responsible for his own actions, unfortunately, Gene was used as a pawn between two much bigger forces than him- Auburn trying to get Alabama. You had a young, disgruntled, down-on-his-luck guy sitting in a room chewing on tin foil saying, 'I should be in the NFL! I should be treated better and taken care of! Alabama had not taken care of me right!' And then people come up and say we'll be taking care of you. Gene has said it's true and he's said it's not true, and frankly, no one knows...

"Ultimately, Alabama paid a price- the NCAA allegations... allegations on Langham compared to other cases- the NCAA came at it and thought: we 'think' you're guilty of this. It looked and felt like enforcement staff came up with something along the lines of 'we're gonna punish you more severely for this than we have anyone else..."

When Judge Warren opened the records in October of 1994 as the case went on, Kreimer argued in open court that Gene's life was now in danger. Jelks said in response that after his little brother's junior varsity football game the month before, someone "fired four gunshots at me" driving by in a car.

Pullen's attorneys wanted to show a relationship between Jelks and Atlanta businessman William "Corky" Frost while, at the same time, court records showed that Stan Kreimer wrote the 28 checks totaling almost $37,000 since Tommy Deas broke the news in his coverage- 26 of those were from an escrow account. The Tuscaloosa News would divulge that the withdrawals for Jelks ranged from $303 to $5,413

Frost had been banned by the NCAA for his role in the Eric Ramsey case. He admitted that he did help Gene out at times. He provided $1500 to Gene so he could purchase some clothing shortly after Jelks came to Atlanta in 1992. In July of 1994, Jelks identified Frost as the person who referred him to Kreimer in the first place.

Corky Frost, when growing up in Alabama, didn't even know an "Auburn" existed. He was in mourning with the rest of the state when Tommy Lewis tackled Dicky Moegle. You could only be what you heard about growing up.

He qualified for state three years in a row running track- even his track coach, Charlie Bentley, played for Bear Bryant at Kentucky.

But Corky ended up going to Auburn on scholarship.

"I guess the reason I fell in love with Auburn was, when I went on my first trip to Auburn for the state track meet my sophomore year, Coach Bentley couldn't find me a room. I had been to Tuscaloosa but the people, the campus, and the atmosphere in general at Auburn, was something I had never experienced.

"I don't know where Coach Bentley stayed, but somebody took me over to the old Bibb Graves Centre where all the athletes stayed. It was in spring quarter & a lot of the football players had gone home for the weekend. They put me in a cabin over there where I could sleep Friday night. The guy in the other side of the cabin was (1958 Outland Trophy Winner) Zeke Smith.

"And these guys took me up to the chow hall- best meal I ever had in all my life. So, when I left there, that's when I fell in love with Auburn. And then, I never looked back.

"When I started learning about Auburn was my 8th grade year when Buster Gross, from our high school, signed with Auburn. He was the first of several. Buster stayed injured most of his time at Auburn. He was a little small and a little too tough for his own good. He was one of the hardest hitters I ever saw in high school. He actually broke a kid's leg from Gadsden High School.

"When I was a sophomore the Beaube twins, who played in the backfield at Sansom, were the beginning of 4 to 5 years of probation for Auburn. Jerry Barnett of BBS Wholesale gave us all jobs. He gave the twins $1,000.00 that they gave to their father- who was the minister at Alabama City Church of God. He went to Coach Miller, our head coach at that time, and the NCAA showed up soon after that. Coach Miller had played at Alabama. They were part of the first probation.

"All that started this vicious circle."

And this was 1956...

The LA Times newspaper, in 2011, reported that an Auburn assistant coach paid twin brothers $500 encourage them to play there which caused the three-year bowl ban. Any further violations could have led to talk of expulsion from the NCAA. The pursuits didn't stop there.

"Then, there was Don Fuell from Guntersville, Alabama. They actually had a private investigator follow him. He played his freshman year at Auburn, but had to play his last 3 years outside the SEC at Southern Miss...he was a great athlete.

"Wayne Profit introduced me to Jerry Barnett for my summer job. Wayne was a running back and a year ahead of me. He also signed with Auburn. His Nephew, Freddie Weygand, also signed with Auburn from our high school. Based on my trips to Auburn- especially the first one- Buster and Blackie Blackburn (a running back a year behind Buster), signed with Auburn. And Wayne, when it was time to decide, knew it was nowhere but Auburn."

And Corky's street was stacked with athletes that would make their mark in the state...

"Kershaw Street, in the back of the mill village, was a great place to have a pickup basketball or football game. Wayne lived in #1, Bobby Warren lived in #3, we lived in #5, and Zack Roberson lived in #7. Zack was an offensive lineman 2 years behind me... Yep! He signed with Auburn. Zack left at the end of one season, married his high school sweetheart and had a great career at Jacksonville State. Bobby Warren stayed in Alabama City and made loads of money with two different motorcycle dealerships.

"My neighbor, Zack's Dad, drives my Dad & me down to Auburn on a Saturday morning with my two pairs of jeans and the little bit of everything else I had. I met Coach Gene Lorendo at football practice and he directed me to my cabin, #5 across from the chow hall. When I went in to my room, I couldn't believe how big it was and that there were only going to be three athletes living there. On the Friday night before, I could lay in bed and touch all three of my brothers- talk about a kid who needed a scholarship. There was, like, 6 inches from the wall to the beds and there was about a foot between the two beds on #5 Kershaw Street.

"My mom & dad slept in one room and my 3 brothers and I slept in the other room.

The one thing that was a common denominator was that there was a time where you had to say whether or not you were for Auburn of for Alabama growing up. When you were born in Corky's time frame, you were for Alabama because Auburn "didn't exist" back then. Auburn may not have existed competitively until the two schools played against each other in the late 1940's.

"I had never heard of Auburn until 1949," he admits. "The day after the game, Zack's brother came back to the neighborhood all cut up from fighting after the Alabama loss. There was a riot in downtown Birmingham from the Auburn win."

A missed extra point by Alabama kicker Eddie Salem was the difference in the 14-13 win.

And then the fighting started as Auburn would win their second game of the year making Alabama finish 6-3-1.

"In my way of thinking, I was nine years old," Frost says, "I was like, 'Why didn't they kill them? It was Auburn.' That was the attitude. Nobody knew Auburn. You were raised in the mill villages knowing only Alabama. And, right now, today, there are folks where it's brought down generation to generation."

Frost has never actually sat down at a family reunion where the game wasn't an argument. Bama beats Auburn and you'll know how the win happened. Both sides of fans remember bad calls from ten years before. Freddie Weygand is remembered to this day for his catch/incomplete pass in the series. There will never be a get together without criticism or defense of a position- whether it's church or a family reunion. There will always be a side taken.

"Remember Auburn had beaten Alabama for a few years in a row until Bear got there," he continues. "The high school Alabama Relays were in Tuscaloosa in the spring of 1958- the time of Bear's first spring practice. Coach Bentley took me down to the meet and also over to see Coach Bryant and the athletic office. I got to shake his hand & talk with him for a couple of minutes while we were there. Looking in his eyes and hearing him talk, I could see why so many wanted to play for him. He beat Auburn in his second year.

"He flipped the switch and it was on from there."

The rivalry grew bigger & bigger each year & is still growing.

And thirty to fifty years later, Gene Jelks would be feeling the rivalry from both sides.

From Mike Fish's coverage of October 11, 1994:

In an Aug. 24 deposition, William D. "Corky" Frost, a Lilburn general contractor who was banned by the NCAA from associating with Auburn because of his role in the case that landed the school on probation, acknowledged several ties to Jelks–including providing him $1,500 cash to purchase some clothing shortly after he moved to the Atlanta area in 1992. Frost said Kreimer later repaid him the money.

Frost said he also loaned Jelks $50 when he showed up at his office this summer. Jelks promised to pay him back the next day, but Frost said, "I haven't seen him since then."

In his 122-page deposition, Frost detailed how he drove to Gadsden in October of 1992 to bring Jelks to Atlanta. The next day, Frost took him to Kreimer's office.

Several weeks earlier, Frost said he received an anonymous call inviting him to meet with Kreimer at his law office. At the meeting, he said Kreimer asked him to transport Jelks to Atlanta.

He also acknowledged that Jelks had taped from his office a telephone conversation with Pullen, though saying he was unaware he was doing it at the time.

Pullen would lose the case at every level of the Georgia court system.

But not before it looked like Gene wanted to do a make-good.

Tommy Deas published a piece for the New York Times newspapers on June 4 where a motion was on the table to add Kreimer (now a "former" Jelks attorney), Frost and "99 John Does" who allegedly gave Jelks money during this time frame as co-defendants.

Tom Cauthorn was quoted from a past conversation he claimed to have with Jelks three months previous. Gene had indicated to (attorney Thomas) Cauthorn that the whole thing was a "scheme" to get Alabama in the same kind of trouble that Auburn had gotten themselves with the NCAA.

"We talked to him in March. He called us and said he wanted to talk to us. It was in that discussion Gene indicated... he wanted to undo the damage to Jerry Pullen and the University of Alabama.

"He said he feared for his safety from Stan Kreimer and Corky Frost. It's a pitiful example of grown men who don't have enough to do with their time. They should go out and get more demanding jobs."

Cauthorn talked about a "civil conspiracy" with Kreimer and Frost wanting to harm Jerry Pullen and that Gene even went to talk to an attorney tied to Harold Simmons. But, two days after the Deas piece and two years after the initial case was brought by Pullen, Judge Warren rendered a summary judgment dismissing the case. It was up to Cauthorn to figure out his next move...

The move took a while to go upstairs in the Georgia legal chain...

From Mike Fish's coverage at the AJC of June 6, 1995:

Jelks' attorney, Jonathan Peters, argued that there couldn't be defamation if the allegations were true. Judge Hunter agreed, saying, "Motive is not really an issue."

Attorney Thomas Cauthorn, who represents Pullen, said he plans to ask the Georgia Court of Appeals to overturn the decision. Cauthorn had hoped the court would require Jelks and his former attorney, Stan Kreimer, son-in-law of a prominent Auburn booster, to reveal the source of their funding. "If they're smart, they won't appeal," said Kreimer, dismissed from the case after he was ruled to be a material witness. "The dog had fleas, anyway."

In May of 1996, the Georgia Supreme Court rejected the appeal of Pullen and would have no more appeals under Georgia law.

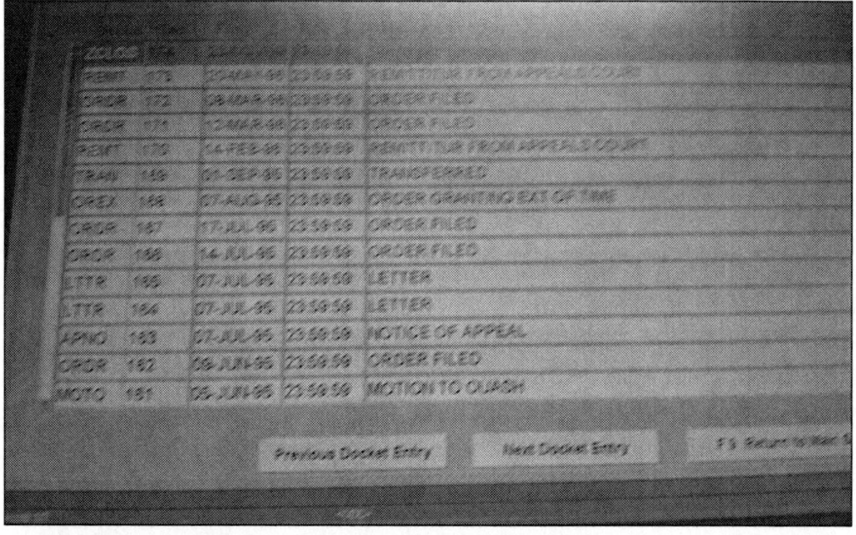

The rundown of the Pullen vs. Jelks court case from beginning to end on a courthouse computer

Chapter 9

THE BEGINNING OF THE END

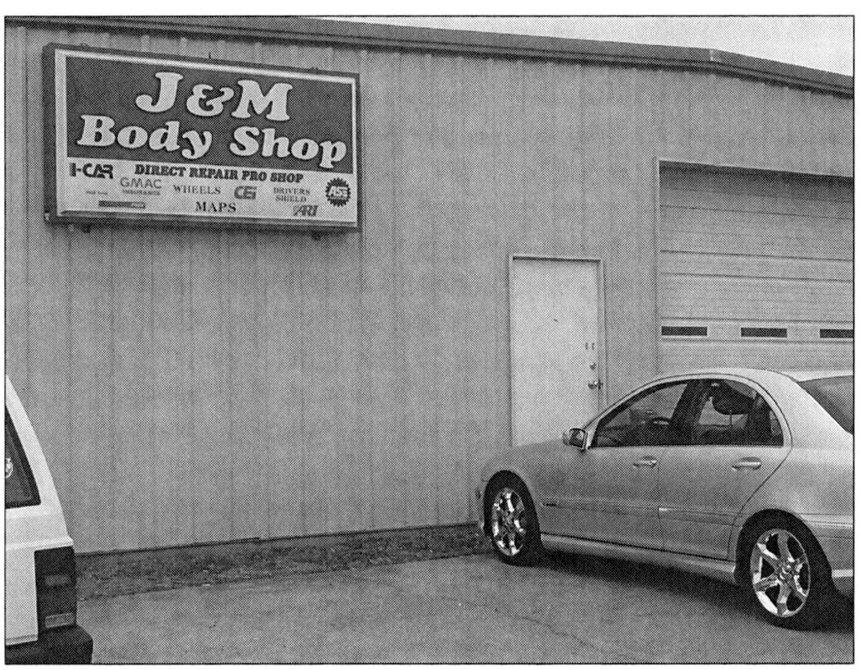

J&M Body Shop in Gadsden: The site of the Pullen-Jelks dust-up

While the trial was going on in 1994, Gene was arrested at the Traveler's Inn in East Gadsden, Alabama on a warrant for writing a bad check at a convenience store. He was released on $1,000 bond. Gadsden Police denied at the time that Gene was "set up."

Gadsden Police spokesman Lieutenant Randy Phillips said they were not even looking for him when they found him. But they also found a crack pipe with cocaine residue in it when he was leaving the room he had checked in to for the evening.

The warrant: Negotiating with a Worthless Instrument

Lieutenant Phillips said that police got a tip telling them that a woman that had an outstanding warrant could be found at the motel. Gene was a bonus. A second woman who was in the hotel room when Gene left was not charged. Warrants charging Gene and the woman he was with added "unlawful possession of a controlled substance" and another misdemeanor charge of "unlawful possession of drug paraphernalia" to the police effort.

No one owned up to the crack pipe. But the police report did say that Gene asked the police officer whether or not they had dusted it for fingerprints. He is reported of saying that he moved the pipe for one of the other two women present and his prints might be on it because of that and nothing else.

After the end of the defamation case in Georgia, it all started going downhill within the next calendar year.

"It was for a four-year period that I was homeless the first time. It had to be around 1996, maybe...I had a lot of demons, a lot of spirits and I was suicidal and ashamed," Gene admits now. "I had worked so hard from 1986 on to be the best. I knew all the odds were against me. I remember vaguely the day that I officially became homeless.

"It was a scary thing not knowing anyone anywhere. Not having money or any of the other resources that were at my disposal at the time coming out of the University of Alabama- which was the number one college in the country. You like to think at the time that if you, pretty much, stay within the means of the NCAA and what they could do for you then, one day, you'll have the opportunity to connect with a lot of people.

"In my case, it reversed.

"That first day I became homeless, I was I believe, in Atlanta, Georgia.

"For someone like me growing up I never knew that side of the track or that life- all I knew was the family, the home, my family home, grandmother's home, aunts, and uncles. I would see people homeless, but I never thought about it. It was like a nightmare. It was a whole different experience for me, not having resources, not knowing what I was going to eat, not knowing where I was going to sleep, no job, nothing, no car...

"I felt empty, embarrassed, ashamed... I would try to hide a lot of the time, but people still recognized me. I kinda camouflaged it. But when the sun hit, I didn't know where I was gonna sleep. Most people went to bed around 10 p.m. I slept in shelters. I slept in the woods, slept on church steps, slept under the bridge. It started to take a chronic psychological effect on me. I just went through the motions like other homeless people did."

But, to live on the streets as Gene did, there are those- much like his time in football- who were the veterans. They had been there for a long time and were not in any kind of place to go forward. Their rules, they knew. So Gene had to learn a new set of rules and obey a different set of veteran teammates.

"They would be, like, my teacher. I observed what they did and, based, on my intellect, so I started hanging around them.

"Most of what I got was when I was first starting out was, 'Are you an undercover police officer?" and I said, 'No, I'm homeless.'

Not that every veteran out there wanted to be a leader for the rookie on the roster...

"There were some mean people out there- evil and mean – a lot of demonic spirits were out there and some would talk to themselves. Some of them jerked and twitched and some of them were with sores on their bodies. Physically, I saw a lot of demonic, dark things that I would have never seen otherwise.

"For example, there were still those eating in nice restaurants and eating in nice places. But I wasn't anymore. I guess it all happened for a reason because it HAD to happen for a reason, I can't explain it. But it was scary out there.

"Sometimes police officers would harass the homeless. And it made me sad to be a homeless person. I once had fame in the sports world- and then to fall down and to shame…??? I guess it was just part of a process that I had to go through. I never contacted anyone for quite some time. My family didn't really know where I was. I would call and tell them I'm okay, but it was a hardship for four years for me."

But Gene is keenly aware of how he made it through those first four years.

"I made it by God's grace through all the hate, the hurt, and the harm. I waited in soup lines, I would wait 'til people would go to lunch in downtown Atlanta on Peachtree Street- hoping that someone would throw something in the trashcan and I would eat it.

"I would pick around and I would eat it. That's how I survived. I would go to Underground Atlanta to wash up. I didn't want to stay in a shelter because I was too scared. I had never seen anything like that before in my life. I really didn't know what I was getting in to. You had to get up at 5:30 in the morning. I had nowhere to go. I did this in the summer, fall, spring, and the winter. It was a terrible experience for me, I don't know if local people or the world knew I went through this. I knew I had to seek help to get back in the world mentally. I didn't know if I was going to get out in the world and die and some people haven't even heard from me in over 20-something years.

"I remember walking down Peachtree Street and a guy pulls out a gun and points it right at my heart and I just fell. I rolled and there was a store maybe 50 yards down. And I knew I was in trouble. My life flashed before me. There was another incident with another homeless person down on Auburn Avenue. I just migrated with them and did like they did, moved around... that's how I survived. I learned all their skills on the street and learned how I survived. But one night there was a guy who pulled a knife on me. He was panhandling cars. I was in his territory..."

And that's not something to cross.

Like those who have property and have built their lives a certain way, the homeless are just as possessive. Since they have lost their previous life, the one that they currently have is one they hold on to that much harder- and they will do anything to hold on to a life that they don't want to lose for another time.

"I was like, 'What are you talking about, guy?' and he pulled a knife on me. I had fear, but at the same time I didn't. I talked him down when push came to shove, I would have taken the knife and I would have stuck him with his own weapon to protect myself. I was in some real dangerous situations. I even stayed where Jimmy Carter built those places on Bankhead Highway a few times. Those Habitat for Humanity homes...??? I was there.

"It's something I don't want to live through again. It's something I don't want anybody to live through. That's just uncivilized for anyone to live through that."

But for those who have been in the shoes that Gene walked in, the decisions are tough- life and death decisions for those who may feel they have no life to live. Family may love the homeless member lost, but if that loved one is indeed a loved one lost, the decisions are minute-to-minute and focused on survival.

Nothing more...

"I would go to shelters, churches, and I wouldn't even eat the food," Gene says. "I almost gagged sometimes. I lost a lot of weight. I got down to, like, 143 pounds at one point. A lot of churches would come around to try and help us when we are on the street. On Saturdays, that's when I would stock up on sandwiches. I would put my hands on whatever I could in the park. That's how I would survive for the rest of the week. Once I would find out information hanging out with other homeless people- where they feed and things like that.

"I would go down to the Georgia State University campus in the park and see what they're doing. I would go to Grady Hospital down the street to use the phone. It's something I don't want to live again."

And, frankly, no one should.

Gene's mother had told him to trust in God and He will fix my life. He would, but Gene would walk through a lot of other struggles along the way.

"I also remember I did accumulate some clothes from churches and stuff," Gene remembers, "and people would steal them. Right from under my pillow in shelters they would be stolen. Some people would get into fights over that kind of stuff. One church at the corner of Peachtree and Pine- I had never seen anything like that in my life... I witnessed a lot of things you would probably see in horror movies, but it was real.

"And by God's grace, I had angels around me. I was not exempt from any of that heartache. There were times when I was homeless and walking downtown and the police stopped me. They said that there was a woman a few blocks down from where they stopped me that said I went after her for money.

"I said, 'I just came from a shelter.' And now I know how some police treat homeless people- not all but some. I have experienced it. They put me in handcuffs and told me I was lying about the situation they pulled me over for. I said, 'Sir, I don't even know where that street's at.' So, I have a lot of bad experiences of being homeless."

But the bottom line for Gene in the end of the 1990's was that Gene felt he made a bad decision. He felt like he didn't have a choice at the time. Nobody would have made a different set of choices, Gene feels, if given the same set of problems. He felt like he was being black-balled. And he was for 19 years. He felt like he didn't have a choice and, then, let his emotions get the best of himself.

He started being hard on himself, so he reached a point in his life where he just gave up.

"I was trying to give up," Gene says with the knowledge of the past right in the center of his thoughts. "I told my mom I was thinking about committing suicide.

"And she said, 'Why don't you just go out onto the freeway and get run over by an 18-wheeler! And go ahead and do that if you want to hurt me! But if that's your choice, then go ahead and do it!"

"I don't want to re-live that again," Gene says. "It wasn't a real good experience."

And that is one of the bigger understatements of Gene's time on the streets.

Gene went toe-to-toe with Bo Jackson as a freshman in the "Iron Bowl," but this dose of reality was something he never saw coming. He felt like it was choice he had to make after he was out of options.

He didn't have a choice, but to disappear off the face of the Earth. He wanted to let whatever he did to Alabama fans, his own fans, or the people that he hurt in general... just to let that stand where it was- it's like not finishing a book. The missing pieces will always be there. But Gene feels that God had another plan for him.

"My mom is a loving kind woman, as are all moms," Gene admits, "and for her to say that – she was always there and my dad was there... they were both blue-collar workers and she loves her kids. She still does. My mom provided the best she could for us, and for her to say something like that, it had to tear her up inside to see me all torn up and mentally confused like I was. And I'll tell anybody, there are good spirits and evil spirits. They're real because I allowed them to come in my body and I was living it.

"It was pretty deep for mom to say that and she got my attention. And I started to be conscious of what she said and I was too cowardly to kill myself at that time.

"I didn't know what it was, but I always sense a good force was there. Actually, I know it was God and Jesus, his son, who had their hands on me in favor, because I'm not supposed to be here to tell this story.

"I'm just not...

"Some 20 years later...? There's no way! I give God all the credit and praise on this one and I tell people God is real. He might not come when you want it. But he will come!"

Gene understands that now- even if it took a while.

"And I'm a living witness to that. He's just a good guy! I had him, but I didn't know who he was at the time. He's brought me through a lot of dangers and situations, and he's blessed me with a lot of good blessings, too.

"I'm not supposed to be here. I'm supposed to be dead.

"I had given up. I felt like I could no longer connect back with the University of Alabama, the program, and the university. That was my life, I put a lot into and contributed a lot to the university and it was my decision. It was taken away from me because of the decision that I made with the scandal five to ten years before. That's something I'm not proud of and I made a mistake. I was angry at Bill Curry. I hurt my family, hurt myself, hurt my teammates, and the brotherhood at the University of Alabama. I hurt the fans, my fans, it's something I had to live with for 20 years.

"And I'm sorry I made that mistake.

There are lessons to be learned and taught in this heavyweight life-lesson, and it applies to a lot more than just a football player trying to get a degree or further his career as a professional. There are people out there who will find your weak spot and try and offer you money. There are people who may cross your path to try and do something bad and all Gene tells anyone who will listen now is to recommend you say 'No.'

"It happened to me once in the sports world, one mistake, and here I was, homeless, rock bottom, and I made a bad decision to accept money from Auburn. It was an opportunity to get even with Alabama and at that time I felt like I was still trying to live that life style...

"I had one really bad night one winter in particular. It was about five degrees one winter night in Atlanta. I had about four blankets on the ground. I had no food... I mean, it was literally hard cold. My body was tired of walking. I was tired of walking miles and miles and miles for food. Finding food through word of mouth that they were feeding people over here and they were feeding people over there... it took a toll over me. I went from dressing real nice to dressing in hand me downs and bum clothes... not being around educated people that I was used to... not being able to have access to technology. Not having access to free will and food... not having access to a bank account, checking or savings, that lifestyle got old and weary. Seeing other people walk to and fro and drive their nice cars that I once had. And I no longer had nothing but God. And some time, the adversary had something to say to me, the devil and I had a choice to make.

"I was walking from Auburn Avenue after hustling at a club washing dishes in the kitchen walking back to Underground Atlanta where my place was under the bridges in the Gulch. I was preparing to go to sleep, but I couldn't because I was hungry- no food nor any hot liquid to nourish my body. I decided to search for food and walk a little further to the railroad tracks near the Atlanta Journal-Constitution building.

"I got up under the blankets I had and I was shivering and at that dumpster by the AJC, I always had 'my place.' That's where the Popeye's restaurant emptied all their food. I kept my ears open and you had to do that on the street to survive and where to find food. I walked down the railroad tracks. It was cold in the marrow of my bones. I didn't find any food. I just found bones and boxes and went through the trash and went through the trash trying to find some kind of nourishment for my body...

"All I found were empty boxes and a bunch of rats.

The Gulch, Gene's base camp when homeless in Atlanta

"I had no food, no way to call my family to come get me. I thought I was literally going to die of hypothermia. A while back, I got up under those covers and I said 'God, you know my heart. I have entertained the world, my family, and the University of Alabama. Because God gave me that talent to help me in this situation. I gave you my heart, my mind, and my soul- just send me somebody because I was hungry. I was scared. And I didn't know what else to do so I cried out to him. With all my heart and the way he made me out of my mother's womb. And I asked him to feed me, send somebody to me, and send me a sign.

"And I'll do whatever you want me to do – no excuses–not religion, not Christianity, none of that. I said speak to me."

He got that sign, but it was in God's time.

"A week later I was still homeless, but he answered my prayer. Some railroad track police officers showed up that night. Flashed the light and they said, 'Do you have some ID?' I said yes, I had just gotten off work. I hustled at a restaurant washing dishes and hadn't gotten paid yet. I was still waiting to get my first check in. I know the policemen weren't from God, they were looking for people who were running scams and it was so cold.

"They said that I could stay down here and tell us information... be an informant and I said no. I said you can go ahead and arrest me for trespassing I have nowhere to go.

"So they told me they were going to let me stay that night and I knew that God had a plan. They had told me about a place down by the Ritz-Carlton Hotel downtown where I could go and seek help and I went. Seek and ye shall find, right? There was a ministry there and there was a white pastor there and I knew it was God. He was doing interviews and he told that I had to come back at 7 that night. I'm thinking to myself, 'What am I going to do between 1 and 7?' Go do this? Go do that? I stayed still and I went back and there were 11 people – potential clients — to get into this ministry in Gwinnett County outside of Atlanta. It was called 'Inspire' I believe.

"The minister interviewed all 11 people including myself and this couple and told me that he would be back in a little while. He came back and said he made a decision. I was the only one he chose of all those people.

"God heard my prayer that cold night and I knew God heard me.

"The minister said, 'Are you ready?' And I said 'Me?' and he said I chose you out of all these 10 people for a year. He asked me again, 'Are you ready?' and I told him that I have all my clothes a couple of miles away at Underground Atlanta and I need to go get my clothes from all the other places and shelters out of my clothing closets from where I was living at the time. I didn't have anything material-wise, but he told me, 'No. Leave everything.' And that's how it began for me.

As it turns out, it was like a transitioning house or a half-way house in today's parlance. Gene had to work in the house's telemarketing office to pay his rent. Being the only person chosen of the eleven in that initial meeting brought Gene's ego back. You know he was walking into the house going, 'I'm Gene Jelks.' But that attitude wouldn't fly. He had to humble himself, but he didn't know how he was going to do it. Gene trusted this pastor and his mission for up to a year.

And, then, he said his time was up. He had completed the program and didn't have anywhere to go. He remembered calling his family and they came out to see how much he had tried to move forward in his life. He pretended that everything was okay and it wasn't. He ended up getting a cleaning job in downtown Atlanta at the Georgia-Pacific building for three years, but then the company who had the contract lost their deal. He got an apartment even though it didn't have any electricity. But he could tell when he looked in the mirror at the end of the day, that he was making progress.

He reached out to God and got his answer- the first answer of many that God would give him along the line. And it took that much effort to get through to 2005 or so...

But remember all the talk about being tested...??? He was tested over and over again...

He wasn't satisfied with his own progress, so he started drinking. And after that, he started using cocaine.

"And that's when the demon really came out," Gene acknowledges. "And there were no drugs in our home growing up, and I was never experiencing stuff like that until I was 31 years old. All I did was train. I didn't drink or smoke or anything. What little odd jobs I got through temp agencies in my thirties, I would drink and use cocaine not to think about the scandal. It was costly. I made a bad choice. I got bad results, so I wanted to numb myself up. Going to detox, it wasn't me. So after that, I was jobless and hadn't had a job since the scandal hit, I couldn't get a job anywhere... nowhere in the Southeast. I moved and a family member suggested I move all the way to California to get away from it.

"Remember, I was being quoted in USA Today and Sports Illustrated. And I woke up that one morning in 1994 and I was watching CNN and I was everywhere. I was all over the news and it kind of freaked me out. I was asking myself at one point, 'What in the hell have I done...?' All because I allowed one coach to get my anger and made it worse. My family told me not to do it. I made a major mistake and I didn't listen. And I regret it to this day.

"It's like a failure on the field," he says. "I had built some stability and had built some foundation and then my foundation was no longer. It had been destroyed. My spirits, and they were dark spirits, were chasing me after the illusion of the alcohol. The cocaine came after that where I found out what a normal feeling could be. But to have the upper... that stimulant... the effect of it was like a sensation, it's a false feeling. I no longer was thinking about the sports scandal and was only thinking about feeling good.

"It was against the normal equilibrium in my body. I didn't like the down side of it, though. You crash and you have no energy. You're lazy and you don't want to take a bath. You don't want to eat. It's a hard feeling like that when your body doesn't want to eat. The cortex in your brain doesn't know what you're feeding off of. And you're taking a chance of having a heart attack and dying and overdosing. Actually, to be honest, I felt ashamed. But my heart was one to give back in my state. My heart was one to make an amends to the University of Alabama and the brotherhood... my guys and my teammates. And so, I wandered in and was thinking that you'll never regain Alabama, brotherhood, or connection with university alumni.

"I just followed the devil and the dark side.

"It felt like the right feeling, the delusional feeling, but in reality it was like a lie. The effect of the cocaine was that it gave me hyped senses, and the alcohol put me in a stimulant position. I was like an upper and a downer.

Gene had a skill when he was a little boy. His uncle made him wash cars. He went to clubs on weekends, and got their credit cards and convinced people to do a "dry rub" for them. It's like doing a dry wash with a bucket of water. He impressed the person in charge at that one club and he got $20 to start washing cars on Auburn Avenue in southeast Atlanta. He started hiring homeless people to wash cars for him creating his own business model helping out others. His territory included the police precinct on Auburn Avenue. But he couldn't keep himself out of trouble and getting noticed at the time. He urinated one morning in the police district while he homeless and the officer caught him.

"He asked me what he should do," Gene says.

"I said, 'Do your job.'

He said, 'No, I heard you're the car wash man.'

I said, 'Wow, you're the guy.'

My ego took over again, and the police officer told me to take a rag, and wipe the car down.

"That's your penalty!"

"It was God," Gene admits. "And so, I started washing their personal cars at the precinct. And I only charged $10. Police officers, off-duty and stuff, I got enough money to get one of those pre-paid phones and started my own little business. That's how I survived and I made good money. I employed homeless people on Auburn Avenue and homeless people would come to me and ask if I needed them:

"Can you use me, car wash man?" they would ask.

"And if they ticked me off and they didn't wash a window right," Gene said, "they were gone. This is my living now, you know. I made good money on it."

But he spent it on drugs and alcohol.

Auburn Avenue District in Atlanta

It was another year until he cleaned it up again. He would stay anonymous. But there would be those moments where he would lose his quiet.

"I remember one of my teammates at the University of Alabama ran into me once," Gene says. "I was parking cars downtown for football games. And learning the tricks of the trade, I ran into one of my classmates. I was ashamed and I kept my head up, and I told him to 'come on in' to the lot I was guarding. I told him that I would watch his car. He knew that I was going through a kind of transitioning and when he came back he gave me $20. So, I started charging $20 a car for future games. I did that so I could even start getting hotel rooms so I could take a shower.

That gets us to 2005- almost a decade on the streets and away from the East Coast after spending a handful of years in California. And Gene, finally, wanted to tackle his chemical demons, face them once and for all, and try to put them behind him.

"I decided to go into a place where somebody told me to go and get treatment," Gene says. "I was just doing it recreationally. But I remember that this one gentleman told me to go and tell this group of people that you need a place to stay because you have a drug problem. So, I did. They gave me free room and board, I just did the chores until I figured it all out.

"So, God did it. He helped me. And I know that. And that's how I lived for a while. I would go from place to place, pretending like I had a problem- even though I really did. I didn't want to sleep in a shelter. I didn't want to sleep in the woods. I didn't want to sleep under a bridge anymore and not have any more five degree nights. I don't want to wish that kind of life even on my enemy.

"But that's how I survived. And I just made up my mind to block the scandal out of my mind and focus. I went home to Gadsden and saw Bishop Steve Smith for the first time in twenty years and decided to surrender it all. He came home and talked to me, and said there is going to be a revelation.

"In 2008, it came true. That was my first official speech.

Chapter 10

RECONNECTING WITH FAMILY

As with most disappearances, when someone decides that the only life they live should be their own and no one else's- regardless of the reason- there comes the time to face those that are the most affected.

For Gene, his time in the woods meant that marriages would dissolve, relationships would dissolve, and he would not be a part of the lives of the most important people to him. To make those steps back as part of his rehabilitation and reintroduction into the lives of those who loved him most, the reaction has been varied- from cautious to unconditional love.

Like Gene's daughter Erica...who didn't know him until her senior year of high school.

"Our relationship now is one of those simple, typical, father-daughter relationships. I didn't meet him 'til my senior year at my high school graduation. There was no 'growing up' relationship.

"You just make the most of it. I forgive him for not being a part of my life. I have nothing against him. I just welcome him into my life with my children as my biological father.

Erica has three children for Gene to be a grandparent to- Alizah McCowan, Khayden Carter, and Zoey Carter.

But their first contact- was awkward. How could it not be so...?

"He came to my high school graduation. I didn't know he was coming. It was a brief visit. Because as a high school grad, I have my own thing planned on that day. He came up to me and was living in California. He came up and I saw him. We took a couple of pictures, and that was pretty much it. He had a gift for me. I left it for my mom to take home, but I went to parties and didn't spend time with him that day.

"That was it.

"I never heard from him again. I reached out to him at one point, now and then, he would be speaking with mom and brother, but he was still in the streets. Eventually, he came back to Atlanta.

"When he reached out the last time, something came into me to see where he was and how he was doing. On the streets, at the time, I think he was still doing drugs. He was living on Bankhead Highway in west Atlanta and I went with two of my kids and visited him. We had a little relationship, but I thought it was too late for me and he and I thought it was something that needed to be done for his grandkids.

"At one point, he ended up going into the hospital. He had some kind of heart attack- maybe something to do with drugs, but he wouldn't admit it to me at the time. I visited in the hospital and he called me while he was in and said he had a heart attack. I broke it to him really honestly. I extended my hand and asked him if he wanted help. He went through the motions and I enrolled him in a drug rehab program. Unfortunately, I found out that he had been in most establishments that had offered those kinds of programs already. We also found out that it was difficult to have a place to take him since there's a time limit to come back once you're out."

Things didn't get much better...

"I got him a cell phone so I could get in contact with him when I needed. I dropped him off again. He started another drug program, and told him where he needed to go. The next day, the cell phone wasn't answered, and I would not hear from him in weeks. He reached out to me finally and told me that someone had taken his belongings.

"I just told him that I don't have to do this- trying to establish a relationship. But I told him that I didn't need to do this. I am fine in the rest of my life not having a relationship. I was going to extend my hand, but I wasn't going to stretch it.

"I asked him not to contact me again until he changed his life and do what he needed to do for himself. There was nothing he could do for me at this point of my life as a father, but a couple of years later, he reached back out. Turned out, it was four years later after the first incident in 2005. In 2009, I reached out to him again in Atlanta as he was working in some cleaning company. He got in touch with my mom and they tried to rekindle what they had. He ended up moving out again with my mom for a period of time.

"And, obviously, that didn't go well. The person I am, when he was leaving the second time, he had nowhere to go. I thought he was clean. I opened up my home to him. I don't know where my trust came from.

"He moved in and stayed for a year. I asked the Lord what I was trying to do since he hadn't found a job. It got to a point where I had to ask him what he was going to do and find out who he is. He doesn't know the 'Eugene Jelks' part of who he is. I told him he has got to let the football part of his life go because that part of your life is dead.

"He only knew himself as that 'character' in a part of his life. He ended up back with my mom again. They tried again and it went really bad. I told him he couldn't come back here, because it wasn't a good idea from the start.

"He went on to move back to Alabama to help take care of his mom. I think he's great guy and very intelligent, but he hasn't found his identity and doesn't know how to just 'be.' He has tried to be himself, but he's a confused and conflicted person. It doesn't come off very well. He tried the persona of someone else.

"He is just in need of counseling and realizing who he is and being okay with it. He doesn't have to try to be a celebrity or some star and being a spokesman for others. I kinda let him know that it's okay to be a regular person. Everybody can't be in the limelight.

"My mom didn't talk to me about him when I was growing up. When she acted out, she would yell about him not being in my life when I was a young child- my adopted grandparents sought a meeting with him. They took me to Alabama and he was supposed to be there. As usual, he came up with an excuse. I didn't know if that was one of his moments, but my mom never talked bad about him.

"I tried to take up for him as I got older, and I wasn't a part of his life at a peak of his football career. But I believe it may have taken priority over a child. I just don't know if there was a disconnect or not.

Has the relationship grown over time...?

"I think it has grown," Erica admits. "He was like a playmate for my kids. My kids love him to death. They enjoy seeing him as a grandparent and I didn't get the time to spend with him growing up, it balances. I accepted the fact of what it is.

But there is that distance that still is there and hasn't healed...

"If I got married," she admits, "then he wouldn't necessarily be the one who walked me down the aisle because he wasn't that father figure in my life.

"I knew over my childhood, he looked like a father figure. But he would be the one over time. He wasn't there, but I can't fault anybody. I don't dread on woulda, shoulda, coulda. But I did tell him that he can't be, like, a daddy to me... He can't tell me what to do in my life. He doesn't know all of me. He would have had to see me grow. He doesn't know the depths of my personality. But I still respect him, and I will put him in his place sometimes.

"I call him my dad. But he's not my 'daddy.' I won't go to him over a problem, because I think he has enough problems as it is. He is more of a friend in that sense.

But what about the future…???

"I am not hoping for much of anything. I am not looking for strong relationship. I am okay with how things are. I am just not trying to force anything.

"I listen to him and he makes me laugh and joke a lot. I tell anybody with power that lived a life as such- being addicted to drugs- that anything could have seen him relapse. I don't know if he has an urge. I applaud him for what he is doing now. I know he wants more out of his life. I just don't know if he knows how to make that happen yet.

"He is not exposed to much schooling. He is just known for athletics. Any other great attributes, no one really knows or sees. He holds onto that because that's the Gene that everyone knows. The regular, old Eugene Jelks doesn't have a fan club and I think it bothers him. He wants people to remember that and I don't think he can let it go.

"Either that or he's trying to let it go and hasn't figured out how. I understand more of him, though, than his football personality."

Dante Jelks- Gene's brother, 11 years younger

"I was, mainly, close to my parents. I admit that I was a daddy's boy, even as I was close to my sister, Audry. We were a close-knit family.

"Gene was strict on me as a child. You want to have your way, but he didn't allow that. He was showing me the right ways, and chastised me in the right way. He was strict on me until college at the University of Alabama. Then, it was different as I craved being around him.

"He was not as strict on me in college. I would call him to get game cheats for Nintendo. He would know the games and I asked about 'Mike Tyson's Punch Out' for cheats from his teammates. He would take me into locker room with him. It was more joyous and more fun.

"He would just make sure I cleaned my room and cleaned around the house. He wanted to make sure that when I played, I stayed in the yard. He was more a help to my father as another father figure.

"It was very electrifying to go into the locker room. Being that young- between 6 and 10 when he went to college and I didn't understand the magnitude of large names. I enjoyed being around guys like Mike Ramil. #92, who was not even a starter. He blocked a field goal in the 1989 game vs. Penn State. I just remember him being real tall (Ramil was 6-7, 260). I was fascinated by him being so tall and just took a major liking to him.

"Ramil was a big name to me. He accepted me like a little brother. I would call and write letters. He called me 'Little Jelks' and 'Little Gene'- he embraced me.

"I thought about it as I got older... how upset Gene was about what happened. It didn't show at the time- at least that side of his anger when I was young. As I got older, I started realizing how manipulative people will be and how important decisions are made – something you never experienced before can be enticing. When you're young and under that much pressure, it can be traumatic mentally.

"I noticed it more in my 20s with the pressure he was facing. Gene had stayed away from the family in my 20s. My dad died when I was 12 or 13 when Gene was living in Atlanta. He wasn't playing football at the time. But around the time of the allegations, he would call and come into town. But that was in my teens. He wasn't around all that much because of his drug addiction.

"Being that young, I didn't understand why he took on that lifestyle. I didn't appreciate it because he had wear and tear on my mother. She cried a lot and took it for the family. Moreso, it was the spirit of the drugs that got to him. You know in real life, Gene wouldn't do that. He is a giving, big hearted person. My mom would be crying and Gene actually took things from me. And I was just not understanding what he was going through. It put a value on material things and made me angry and frustrated.

"At times, it made me fearful for him and didn't want to be afraid.

Gene took a radio, a television, and some of Dante's money- that's what he could remember that went missing during Gene's dark time.

"My brother, Anthony," Dante continues, "it was hard to read him a lot of times because he is dealing with stuff internally and you won't know he's dealing with it. My sister was hurting too. We were closest and right next to him in age. She never showed any tears or what have you. She brought out a defense mechanism and knew the real person he is. My brother didn't show it to her. At the same time, they were all trying to talk to Gene and get him guidance as well as into rehab.

"What I think it says, from a spiritual point of view, is that for the same individual, for Gene, to have gone through all of this and to still have the same joy and motivation to do better- speaks volumes more than I can express verbally.

"I am a funeral director these days. I saw Gene get caught up in it and saw him overcome the good and the bad and still keep pushing. I can't express how powerful that is and how amazing it is and it shows that, at the time, he was dealing with problems. The real Gene was still trying to persevere. He was continuing to fight and not only to save himself but others. I think it says he's not a selfish person.

"I think he's still a role model- after all the death threats, and people turning their backs on him, and denial of job opportunities and overcoming that, now, people communicate with him. He is willing to help in any form or fashion. I think it says a lot about his character.

"Gene as he's gotten older, he has become very talkative. I love my brother. Sometimes he gets on your nerves, but I appreciate and enjoy him. I would rather him talk to me to death than live the lifestyle he was living. I would rather he do that than anything else. And to see him be active in the church...? I admire his way of getting to powerful individuals and how he gets to them. He still has that mind of acceptance.

"The moral...? Never give up, never give in. Because if he had done either one, the story to this point, wouldn't even be anything. It would be an average story- no different than anyone else's, just another number. The life he has lived and the things he has overcome, it says miracles still do happen.

Audry Montgomery- Gene's sister, a year younger

"Living in Gadsden was interesting," she admits. "For me, it was three brothers, and a little hectic. I was the only girl. Dad was real protective and would get me everything I wanted. Gadsden was not really country or city, there was not a lot to do sometimes, but it was nice.

"Some teachers would treat me a little special because he was a good football player. If I was caught in the hall without a hall pass, I didn't really get in trouble. They wouldn't say anything. They may stop someone else and send them to the principal.

"I was in the band, too. I played clarinet when he played trumpet. He was really good. And when he was on the field in his football uniform- it was pretty funny. You could ask anyone in the state of Alabama and they would know about Emma Sansom football at that time in the 80's.

"The town was unified, and they were so proud of the team being from Gadsden. Everyone was unified and they wanted to be a part of that. The town produced star athletes and football teams. All the players were best of friends. They didn't allow race or anything to divide them. They were more of a family.

"There were a lot of people still who held the old ways in their hearts as things are passed down generation to generation. But nobody said a lot about it. I worked with a woman who constantly reminded me she had a grandfather who worked on a plantation.

"But it was crazy when he was being recruited. We were always invited to games all over the place. There were players who were now pros try who would try to entice you. They would tell us, 'We would like to have you come here as well.' It was crazy and fun. I had always loved football. I was a tomboy, and

I always have enjoyed it. To see them play and be that close to it was fun. But it was kind of exhausting. There was a football game on Friday and then we were off to a college on Saturday. And it was several colleges- Auburn, Alabama, LSU, and we even went to UGA. There was always somewhere we were going.

"And, yes, I remember when Ozzie Newsome called. Yeah, he hung up on Ozzie.

"I think he always knew he was going to Alabama. It was always something in his heart he was going to do. He was wonderful as a freshman. He was kind of a different person. A lot of things don't impress me. For me, going to a game was wonderful because it was football. Then, I remembered my brother was out there.

"Football is religion in Alabama. Being on the football team was another type of religion- with how the fans are and the team, boosters, and alumni are. It definitely was a learning experience.

"That 'Iron Bowl" his freshman year, I remember I actually saw Bo Jackson on the way into the game. There were interviews before he was even to get into the locker room. People were yelling at him he was going to do so well and he just smirked and kept walking.

"After the game, this freshman outdid Bo. It was unbelievable.

"But when he got injured, it was difficult for him. He was always used to excelling. And to not even be able to get on the field, it was hurtful to him. He went to a dark place for a minute. He wanted to show people what he was capable of, but when you're injured it's kind of difficult.

"But what people don't understand is the thing where there was a little daylight...? He and Bobby Humphrey are such good friends. It was hard on Bobby as well. I feel like they didn't want to compete against each other. Bobby felt he wanted to be in a position, and Gene felt like he wanted to be in a position.

"They were friends and didn't want to go against each other. They were used to running the ball and used to making big plays. It was a difficult thing. Gene was capable of playing defense, it was just not what he wanted to play.

"Of course, all you heard was the politics of it all- about alums encouraging and even doing things maybe even unethical to make sure Bobby was the running back.

"It was just people using the power they have. We all know that money is power. Were they using the power...? I have no proof or evidence of that. I know that's what the talk was.

"Because I was his little sister, I was a tomboy and I tried to follow him around. But I was a girl, and a lot of his friends were attracted to me. It became a problem. He didn't want little sister trying to do boyish things.

"When things got bad, I knew what had gone on. I didn't want that publicized because it effected more than just him still living in that town. He would and we all would get different looks and people were treating us differently,

"When he was gone, we had totally separate lives. I didn't know what was going on except what my mom was telling me. She would say that Gene called. He's not in a good place right now. As far as knowing what was going on with him, I didn't really know. I was just concerned with his well-being.

"I couldn't reach him, but at the same time, people have to want to be helped.

"My mom hurt very much from that time in his life. We wanted him to be well. All parents want a better life for their kids, but it is hurtful even more since there was nothing he could do- and nothing we could do.

"We got back in touch with each other for the first time five or six years ago. Gene had always said to me there was reason we didn't get along, and that was that I knew him better than anyone else. So I knew when he wasn't telling the truth or living the way he was supposed to. I could look past it and tell that he was lying.

"But, now, he's such a better person. He is a loving uncle. He calls to check in and asks about granddaughter. He has a relationship with my son. He is trying to rebuild his family and he is a happy-go-lucky person now.

"He has life in his eyes.

But, with everything he has done, how hard is it to forgive someone who left- left for a very long time, and is only recently coming home...?

"It's extremely easy," she says. "I don't care what he does or where he goes, he is still over there. Our family has been taught to help each other regardless of what's going on, the love was never lost. He has worked hard to regain people's trust and make his own life better. I am proud of him for that. We try to get to him regardless and remind him to work hard now to be a person he wants to be now, because we can see it and the person he can be is in himself.

"The process isn't difficult. I know Gene for Gene before he became running back at Alabama, and I think it's easy for them to see Gene again in the way he is now...

"There are alumni who may have turned their backs, but they're taking to him now. He's communicating with family now. It's not difficult for us, because we knew who he could be and who he was before the turmoil. So, it's not difficult.

"I know that there are always people who will not forgive. But if you're going to be healthy, the idea is to look past this. If they can't forgive you, then that's on them…

"From our perspective, you've done your part if you're Gene. People may see it as something not ever forgiving him. But we were brought up in the church. God can forgive him. He still has a life that he has to lead. He is trying to compensate for things he did and he is trying to do ...what he needs to do…to get where he needs to be.

Anthony Jelks- Gene's brother

"We had a wonderful family life growing up. We had great parents. They brought us up right. But they chastised us when we needed it. They bought things for us when they could, and we had a good life. Although, I was chasing women when Gene was playing football since we have a two year age difference.

"To see him succeed on the field was exciting. I went to some games. And as long as there wasn't a female on the line, it was cool. A lot of times I was at the game, I was chasing women. But it was cool to be at the games.

"I was part of the training staff when Sansom won their title. It was wonderful. The Colbert County game in the quarterfinals (a 10-7 win), now that was a game! We were down. And everyone was saying that 'we got this far.' And all of a sudden Gene came out and they couldn't catch him.

"Because of those of us at Sansom- it was a great year. Toney Tolbert is right about that. It was like a family. They hung out, but Coach Gross knew there were some things none of us tolerated. They had to get along like a family. They might get into a fight at practice, but the notion was that we get together at the end of the day- and, then, we would wonder what we were fighting about.

"And, then, Gene goes to the University of Alabama... Frankly, I didn't want him to go to UF because I was a diehard Florida fan.

"Tell you something, though, I didn't see the run against Auburn in the 'Iron Bowl.' I was in a deep conversation with someone on the side of me...

"If you understand what I am saying...

"But as he got older, he would call me and I would call and check on him. Some days it would be, 'How you doing?' and that's it. I am not really a phone person like our father was. I would say what you're gonna need to say and get off. I don't have time to call and get caught up with pity stories. I was more of a face-to-face guy for times like that, but phone calls were never on that kind of level. You know, going all the way back to talking about childhood days, I was not the person to bring pity parties to...

"And because they weren't phone-callers, when things got really bad for Gene, Anthony found out a different way.

"I find that out on the news. It was me and this young lady, and that's when I found that out. I wasn't around him, and everyone was saying the allegations were true... that there were no lies in it. That was what the folks were saying in the interviews and they kept saying it was true. My parents worked, and did a wonderful job in raising us.

"We were concerned when the allegations came out. I would try to encourage him that there are better ways to get around this. I tried to motivate him. Because when you look down the road, it took a toll and there's a better way around it.

"These days, I stay encouraging him. I am a pastor also at the Lively Hope Missionary Baptist Church. I am grateful and excited for him. If anyone will admit, when some drift off, some never come back. Gene is one of the fortunate ones. God told him that he had a chance to stay straight and focus on Him.

"The lesson from my point-of-view...? You cannot drown your sorrows in yourself, your goals and feel that way when you don't succeed. Don't give into peer pressure. Keep your mind and spirit focused. There's another door that can be opened for me.

"He wasn't successful on the football field. That may not have been Gene's ministry. I firmly believe that you have a ministry and God has used him with what he went through. Gene has a ministry and story to tell. I stress this to a lot to people. You can't talk about what you haven't been through.

"No one can talk about what you have been through unless they walk a mile in your shoes

"I am very proud of him and excited. You see how you can change. But, there is a point in your life where you have to have a desire to change.

"All you have to do is look at him and see that he is very excited.

Ray Perkins- Former Alabama and NFL coach, now coaching high school football in Mississippi

"Gene is one of my guys. He was one of my guys when we signed him. He was one of my guys when he played. He's one of my guys now.

"I love him. That's just the way it is.

"I am sure he has gone through a lot more than we could ever imagine- from what I understand. I am familiar with the accusations and I know these accusations are not true. They are just not true. Why he would do that? I do not know. I don't think he knows, to be honest.

"But believe me, he is very, very, sorry. He is deeply sorry.

"People ask, 'Why are you with Gene?' Well, he's one of my guys. Even if it was true, which is wasn't, he would still be one of my guys. He'd still be one. I don't know how I would feel about myself if I can't reach down inside myself and find forgiveness for him.

"It's a tribute to him. If he doesn't want to come all the way back on his own, he is not going to get it done. He seems to be determined to do it. And I will help him.

"It makes me proud that he is willing to do it. I'm still looking like this like a coach. I want some hard evidence. And he knows I will say that. I am proud, though, that he is stepping forward.

"One of these days, you're going to see a different Gene Jelks. It may not be this year. It might be a few years from now, but he will be different.

"I believe that!"

Chapter 11

THE ROAD BACK BEGINS

Sometimes, the simplest act and appearance can get a life on track. For Gene, it was reconnecting through a church and their members...

"Going to Bishop Steve Smith's church in Gadsden- I faced the fear and shame of going back no longer being a star. I didn't know God was transitioning me from the world I was in at the time, making sure I was reminded that I was serving Him and belonging to Him. I know he's taken away from all my sins and fear. I was ashamed before I went home. I was excited that I get an opportunity taking me back to the beginning at Underground Atlanta about to freeze to death.

"God had a hand on me showing me favor working behind the scenes. I was walking by physical means and not by faith. And to go to my first speech in 2008, from fame to shame and homelessness, the anointing of it was so powerful. I embraced it and wanted it. I still am just as committed today as I was then.

"The church was packed out on a Saturday. I had four people at the bus station waiting on me and it was just the beginning. We all had great stories that day. I was the guest speaker of all the ministers, and I discovered that this is what the Lord was having me do –running with the second half of my life. And I am going to run it to the best of my ability and I'm going to take this Bible as my playbook and I am going to put on my dress shoes like my cleats and I'm going run for you.

"You don't just force people to find their way, but when an opportunity opens itself up like in football... when a hole opens up, and you have the world class speed, you see the chance to get a quick 6. Today, now I do that by helping get people souls saved, it's amazing how those people showed me love. They didn't know my story at that time, they thought I was still the star football player at the time. They played the "Iron Bowl" on the big screen for that first speech and we still remember it today.

This congregation didn't even know what I was going through, it wasn't time for me to reveal the story. After the speech, the pastor was giving you a love offering of $100. From then on, I decided I was always going to do righteous with it. I remember asking one of the deacons to come up here and I turned around and blessed a kid. I asked God then that if He continued to let me do this I'm going to bless a kid.

That first speech where Gene gave back he got nickels, dimes, fives, ones, tens, and he admits that he didn't have enough pockets to carry it all. People were helping him as it was all weighing him down. He was used to money, but this money was so different, it was God's money. It wasn't car wash money. It wasn't football money. It was money from God. He blessed his family with it and kept $40 from his first speech, and now I know that I had arrived in the next drive of his life, it's about giving back and not handling money. It's about giving back to his family...

"I am here today to serve and to help.

"I fell all the way down to the lowest point you can go to- either the Dead Sea or Death Valley. You name it, I was there. But my message is: There's hope and don't give up. You have got to forgive yourself first. Trust god and the doors that open are there for you. There's nothing that could ever turn me."

He did return to Tuscaloosa after the tornadoes of April 27, 2011 to give back however he could. And the Goode family was instrumental in trying to get him back into the Brotherhood he wanted to be a part of for so long:

"I kept trying to figure out what was going on," Chris Goode admits. "And I think he was looking at his change from running back to defensive back. We talked about it a few years ago, and I think he had a lot of bitter feelings and there were things he needed to do and think about whether it was true or not true. I never asked him why he did it. I think it was just hard times. I think when he hadn't made it as a running back in the NFL and he felt like he still needed to be a running back and he felt it happened at Alabama.

"People knew... I had heard people say stuff about him being homeless. When I heard that, I would ask, 'Do you know how to get in touch with him...?' If you know that, then someone knows he's homeless. The first time I knew he had talked to him was when I was coaching arena football in Birmingham. I started doing that with Bobby Humphrey around 2002/2003.

"At that game, he told me was coming to see us, after the game I saw him. I went up to him and hugged him. I said 'Make sure you take care of yourself.' After that, it was probably another two years and talked to Kerry and we had a long talk on the phone. When Coach (Nick) Saban got here, they got all Coach Perkins' players together. We talked briefly. And it made him feel good that they invited him to the thing.

"I think we kinda, to be honest, I never even thought of it that way- him lashing out. He thought it was something he needed to do. If he's doing what he's thinking is right I wasn't digging into it, and I think it was one of those things. That he played football with us and hangs around and to go back and do some of the things he did. I never would have thought of a guy to do that to a school – right or wrong.

"That's the same thing I did and forgave him "

Gene says these days that he doesn't even watch sports on television and is looking to grow more. He doesn't have a lot of money these days, but if you ask him, he does have it all. He does football clinics in Gadsden and Birmingham to give back to kids these days to make sure they learn from his own lessons as a young man- never to repeat them.

Gene will tell you that you want to be in the kingdom of God- starting on these days on this Earth, and he is a witness now to all of it. And there are all kinds of stories he can tell about his time and all kinds of support groups that help students and student-athletes along the way. The name attached to the campus doesn't matter. It's only the support they give that can help us all grow as adults.

But, Gene will also be the first to tell you that God is in control of it all.

It's all about forgiveness- forgiving yourself, forgiving all those who you feel have wronged you over time so we all can move forward in our lives, and forgive so you can follow in the thoughts of Him as to how your live should be led."

You have to put in the work and it won't be easy to overcome your struggles to get The Prize.

"I realize it was God taking me through the fire," he acknowledges, "and He was in the fire with me so I would not get burned. God is an amazing God! All the glory is His! We are all sinners saved by Grace and we'll need Jesus!"

There has to be trust in God and a belief that He wants you to be in a higher place- that He loves us and wants to work miracles in our lives...

If we only move out of the way and let it happen... And this is for students, student-athletes, and adults...

"If you are the best at what you do, it doesn't matter what that is..." Gene says looking back on his time in the woods, "you can have the prettiest girl, but if you don't have a relationship with Jesus, you could lose your soul.

"I had to experience being stripped of everything in order for God to use me for His plan and purpose... and to listen to His voice for instruction in my life. My desert was like Moses. I had to be alone. But being homeless for all that time I felt alone. But God was right there the whole time burning off my old ways and beginning to plant new ways in spirit for His glory."

Before everything happened in Tuscaloosa, Gene thought he had it made in his life as he thought. But his first lesson of many is that when you're pushed out of a career path, don't get angry to the point it makes you sin. It could cause you to get out of favor with people. But know for yourself, as Gene does now, all you need is favor with God.

The only thing he complains about just shy of 50 years young is the physical nature of his work.

Regardless, everything is lining up in his life now from his perspective...

"I was told when you're sick, you go to the elders of a church, and they will pray for you," Gene says. "But the Bible does not promise that everyone will be healed by Jesus' stripes and that we will be healed. The book of James talks about salvation more than healing. It's in James, John, Acts, 2nd Corinthians, Mark, Isaiah, and Psalms.

"So, I take from that The Father heals who he wants to heal. Man does not have the power to heal, but The Father has all the power and gives man the power to glorify His Holy name. Brothers and sisters, I am just being a witness for Almighty God. I encourage you, if you have not repented, to turn from sin and confess to God that His son Jesus died on the cross for our sins and believe that in our hearts. If you do not, then do so, because the wages of sin is death and there will be eternal death."

For Gene as he moves forward, there will be no more turnovers. It's a different level of responsibility.

It's not about getting a quick 6, it's a long sustained drive.

It's a beautiful thing.

Chapter 12

THE LESSON

In doing the research for this book, the last question asked of all the interview subjects was: "What's the lesson or the moral here?" The answer varied- depending on who you asked...

Chris Mohr

"I think he was dealt a bad hand, and he wasn't able to recover. So, he was going to take out his animosity on all of us and get back at Coach Curry. You know, when you come out with stuff like that, it affects the entire university. And with Curry not there to take the punishment, it was almost like you were cutting off your hand to spite your face.

"I think there was a better way to handle the situation. Go and talk to him... tell him you're not happy... transfer... all this comes from one decision. I think he was intimidated to accept the switch. It's one thing to come and say all that stuff. But you need to come and explain why you said what you said and ask for forgiveness.

"I forgive him. We were all young then. Now that you're older it's like thinking about something in your past and saying: "I can't believe I said or did that." We all have those times in our lives.

"He went through it with us... I forgive him..."

Cornelius Bennett

"I hadn't seen Gene, and then we saw each other for the first time in over 20 years.

"They had Perkins' four-year guys come back a few years ago to spring practice. I had no idea what was going on with him, and when I heard it was shocking. Whether he took something or not, it's the kinda thing that nine times out of 10 it's something you take to the grave. It's between you and God. When it came out, you hear a little more and a little more... and then you hear why... he was down on his luck... Looking at it, do you fault him? Somebody preyed on him. I don't fault him per se because he wasn't in the right state of mind at the particular time.

"Do I forgive him? Hell, yeah, I forgive him! Did I hold it against him, no? Again, that's coming from a brother standpoint. Was I disappointed in him? Yeah. But I've been disappointed in my blood brothers before and I have forgiven them before I go to sleep at night. I'm a different dude. I'm a different cat, y'know...???

"When I saw Gene a couple of years ago, I hugged him, and asked how he was doing, he was honest and blunt in telling me how he was doing, and it wipes away 20 years. Almost 20 years, we were in, out, up, and down, I'm the last person to try and judge him. He's never been on the outs with me. There was never a time, even in the hard parts in all of it, that I would have never turned by back on him. There might be a few guys that would have done that. But I guarantee you deep down inside, everyone that knows what we went through in that lower gym in Coleman Coliseum, that's the separation of the University of Alabama and other universities. But I know from my generations that went through the off- season is that we went through the off-seasons, and the bonding. There's no way in hell you turn your back and would say 'he's not my brother!'

"My understanding is that he reached out to the university family, people turned their back on him and whatever and next thing you know 'boom' we're sitting here talking about it. All I can think of is freshman year, his TD against Auburn, his little Escort- his stereo system cost more than the car. My great memories, I don't even think about that.

"That big smile, y'know...? When his little eyes get small, I always remember him being on the go trying to get somewhere, being from Gadsden. He always was a good kid, and respected the hell out of me. He was always a great kid, loved him to death..."

Kermit Kendrick

"I remember Kerry Goode, either in an e-mail or text saying that Gene was in Atlanta and needed help. I talked to Gene once during that time. I next talked to him three Thanksgivings ago after I called his mom when I was in Gadsden. His mom forwarded my number to gene and we spoke in 2010, I haven't really had a heart to heart with him about why he did what he did. At this time, It just doesn't matter. All of this happened more than twenty years ago. I spoke t him several times since he has moved to Birmingham. He seems to have his life moving in a positive direction.

"I don't know if he feels that he made a mistake or not. I do not think I would have made the same decision were I in his shoes. But whatever happened, however it happened, hurt his feelings. He obviously was in pain. He seems to have found peace with himself and it's good to see the old Gene: joking, laughing, and full of life.

"As long as he wakes up to a new day, he has a chance to write his story and define himself.

"Accordingly, I think the Gene Jelks story is still being told. We know that he showed up in Tuscaloosa without fanfare to help people in need after the 2011 tornadoes. He didn't seek the publicity, the publicity found him. He is hosting football camps in Gadsden. He is speaking at local high schools. He is showing the world that no matter what mistakes you make, you can make a positive contribution. I do not see Gene's life as a tragedy because he is still living.

"He is still writing his story.

"How do you teach young people about acting without thinking through the consequences? Whatever happened to him at Alabama made him angry and he apparently sought revenge. I think one of the key lessons to learn from Gene Jelks is not to react in anger.

"Count the costs before lashing out.

"His life isn't over yet: The lessons for him to learn about himself and lessons for him to teach others.

His character is still evolving. I am happy that he is moving in a positive direction.

So I don't think we can define it right now…

Is that fair…???

Chris Goode

"He thought it was something he needed to do. If he's doing what he's thinking is right I wasn't digging into it, and I think it was one of those things. That he played football with us and hung around and go back and do some of the things he did. I never would have thought of a guy to do that to a school – right or wrong.

"That's the same thing I did and forgave him. During the time I didn't see him, I haven't talked to him or seen him. And when guys stay away like that, you think he's really feeling bad about himself. And when you go through what you go through in lower gym, all you gotta do is talk.

"It is what it is... it was in the past, you know...

"I was telling him always... hey, I think you're telling everyone your faults. And admit to it and not cover it up – some guys will accept it and some that won't believe in God and people will come back around you and talk to you more. Shake your hand... you see people, just be honest with them. It's the best you can do, let them know what you're going through.

"Fans and teammates, when you win national championships, people forget this stuff. If times were bad, other players that had other hiccups, they'd blame it on that. People, if we were being investigated and times were tough, then I think people would remember more.

"All of us go through things, and as long as we're honest by what you did do, raise our hands, and apologize and say we're sorry... if you can forgive him, that's fine, but if you don't then, I understand. And Gene did that and he's done things to change his life around where there's been guys that did a lot of things wrong–no one is free from issues, I found that out with teammates in the NFL. Gene talks about it, things may be true some may not be true.

"He's changed. I'm happy and I'm glad for him. He's turned his life around and I think that's one of the best things. We've had guys who have had problems and turned their lives around- substance abuse and things- Gene went through all phases... how low can you get...?"

Jackie McNutt

"He is trying to do real well and he rubbed the feathers of a few people and they're not gonna forgive him. I said to a few people, if you can't forgive him, don't ask God to forgive you. That's the bottom line. Because you can't ask God to forgive you, if you can't forgive others, can't hold grudges and have them control my life. Gene is a good person and got caught up being alienated because of Bill Curry.

"People turned their backs on him, a lot of them- one that still holds the biggest grudge is Jerry. His brother Joey likes Gene. But I am not going to throw him to the wolves- know someone before you talk about him. When he got hurt, he got on the drugs. He let the drugs get to him. He didn't have to live under a bridge...

"I told Gene: Everybody has problems, the very rich and the very poor. The world is what you make of it.

"A boy crying for help is the lesson in all of this. This is the path God sent Gene down. It was Gene's will, but God sent him down this path. It was just like Jonah and he got back up. This is the path Satan chose for Gene and Gene took him up on it. He walked that valley. He climbed that mountain in the shadow of death. He cried out one night. God picked this kid up out of the ashes and sent him up on the right way. Different people have different lessons. God put me up and sent me down some paths. I came from a bootlegging family. I don't like drugs, but I love racing. My grandmother, aunts, uncle, mother's brother ran whiskey, but I don't like drugs at all...

"I have never kicked him to the curb. He might have a good suntan, but he's got a good heart. There's no color in heaven, he's like my son and I'll cry with him."

Mike Fish

"It's about grown men, adults, fathers, professional people, who have nothing better to do and are so consumed with their college football team. It makes sense if you're a season ticket holder, but if you stoop to this level so consumed in young people playing sports and go to these lengths. I don't understand people stooping to these levels being so consumed..."

Ray Melick

"I would see him from time to time. Auburn people used him. Alabama fans couldn't embrace him because they didn't trust him. You could look at (Antonio) Langham. He could come back. I don't know if they would accept Gene. He sold himself out in the episode to Auburn. Personally, I like Gene a lot. He is a smart young man- it's one of the great tragedies wondering what the full potential of Gene might be. It might have been a blessing, and it might have been a rougher thing. Knowing what he dealt with, it is a shame we didn't get to see full potential as an athlete."

Dr. Gary White

"I think Gene is making a lot of effort to mend a lot of his past ways. I think he's been doing a good job of it. He's making a super effort to be back in the Alabama family and mend relationships. Because any time you do some of the things Gene did and broke a lot of relationships, and you have to go through a time to mend them, some of the players and some of the fans- I'm sure, have not forgiven him.

"Personally. I have…

"I'm a Christian and I believe in what God says to forgive people and forgive him, and we've moved on. Over time, Gene came to me and asked for forgiveness and has since tried to help mend fences that were torn down. I hope through this process and time that they'll all be mended. But we don't know that... with all the fans and players, ex-players or whatnot.

"I wish that Gene had come and talked to me. I thought we had that kind of relationship–that he felt open enough to talk to me about things because we had talked about his feelings. I felt like that if he had come and talked to me that he could have seen things in a brighter manner because I don't even know all what he was going through and what was bothering him that would cause him to do this. On the surface, he said some things, but we have not sat down and talked through and discussed it to talk about what he was going through in his life at that time.

"I had heard he was in Atlanta, but that whole time I didn't know how to reach him and he never made contact with me. I don't know if he had contacted anyone at the university of not. If he did, I never heard about it.

"It was an overwhelming job to handle, but at the same time, God was strengthening me and seeing me through it. We were doing everything we could to clear our name. To this day, the NCAA never proved anything. It was a long and hard process."

George Baker

"He didn't want to dwell into it — you just leave it alone, because the last time you talk to someone you don't want to leave with a negative. He did admit it was a mistake. He was welcome back by me. I was joyful when Freddie Weygand, Ed Scissum, and all of them got together at Etowah High School for a camp. Larry Rose and all of the others all got together and forgave him and he participated in it. I like to see that. They're burying the hatchet. Because if you don't make him welcome to his home town, you got to bury the hatchet sooner or later.

"I feel that in the Alabama die-hards, there will always be in their minds even if they won't say it. I think he's comfortable now to come home to Gadsden now, that's progress you know..."

Toney Tolbert

"He felt like he had let everybody down, I guess. A few years after that, when he came out of his shell, it was good to see him.

Everybody counting him out, but he's coming back, this whole town was behind him. I mean this whole town... he was it...

"After they threw him to the curb, it was just... I dunno...

"It just like I would go into a lawyer's office... you would see pictures in a lawyer's office, but after Gene, then all the pictures were taken off the walls. There wasn't nothing... and you mention it, they change the subject right fast... I can't imagine what he went through getting treated like that. The same people that pat you on the back, kick you in the behind, y'know..."

Eddie Nichols

"Gene came back to Gadsden about a year-and-a-half ago- I will never forget. 'Man of God,' he said, 'This is Gene Jelks." And that was so profound from him. I could tell he had changed and I knew I had to get with him.

"You find out where God's got him going and, at the same time, Gene needs to realize that some people are not going to forgive him. Where does forgiveness come in this whole thing? When I told people I was going to help his clinic, people would ask, 'Why would you go and do that?'

"How many years ago was that? Some people have the mindset that is so crimson and white, they can't let it go. The word of God says: 'Who art man? Thou art mindful of it.' He is on a new journey and a new path. You walk on past those negative people. He has nothing to be ashamed of- he is never going to win them back. The only person to change their heart is God, you can't change others.

"I don't want him to get discouraged. I knew it had to be a certain way. I just encourage him in his different walk and trust God will get you through it.

"I think the lesson here is- when you come to a point in your life, where you are so dependent on university and man, it is all temporary and it will all let you down. I am at a place in my life where my dependency is on God.

"As the Bible says: Fix not your eyes on the things that can be seen, fix your eyes on what can't be seen...

"Because the things that can be seen are temporary- things can't be seen are eternal. That's the lesson- what you're involved in now is the eternal. What you were involved in was the temporary. Those things – name, recognition, yardage, all that stuff is irrelevant- it will pass away. The impact you make for Jesus Christ, the things you and I can't see and we step out in faith- and realize the journey God has for us will last in eternity."

Gene Lett

"I didn't know what was happening with him until I saw him when his father died. He wouldn't say or talk about it, but we have become close ever since. We have been rocking and rolling along.

"He has the determination in the inside to accomplish what he puts his mind to. He had a heart, and was determined to come back after he gave his all. He came back for us here in Gadsden from the downfall in his life. I take my hat off to him and what he's been through and the stand he's making now.

"After the downfall, I didn't treat him differently. Everybody here loves him.

"He wasn't giving up when it got bad for him. He, probably, gave out but he wouldn't give up. That's him."

Walter Smith

"We spent a year, a year-and-a-half out of touch. I would see his mom and dad and always ask about him and pray for him. 'When I asked for him, if I had ever been given the chance to give one of those heart to heart talks, I would look at him and tell him that we all face awkward situations–sometimes at the same time, it would take a lot to have the courage to face them. When he began to face some of the circumstances that he found himself in, we have to understand, sometimes you don't have the total right, mindset at that time to deal with the matters you have.

"As you mature and grow, you handle things in a different matter.

"We were 'just like us' reconnecting after all that time. I had played football all my life before I got injured at the University of

North Alabama. It got to a point I couldn't stand to watch a game, but as times went by-I was able to overcome that. I am thankful that Gene got himself to a place to overcome the drugs. I think one of the most key factors in his moving on is him developing with Jesus Christ. "In this life, you'll have trials and tribulations. You keep good cheer and you'll overcome the world. When we don't have the right influences, gather with someone who has our best interests at heart. Be cautious on saying 'yes.' 'Yes' is a powerful statement when you don't know what's involved in the yes you're saying- it's big learning the difference in where to put the 'yes' at and where to put the 'no.'

"It's a tough thing to figure out. This journey God has allowed us to walk in? Gene became bitter, troublesome, and worrisome. After all that, things are turning around.

"I am thankful I got to be a part of his life to encourage each other no matter the distance. We can always talk and communicate with one another."

Tommy Wise

"I always felt like he was getting a raw deal. The biggest issue- the way I heard it, Coach Curry said we need him on the other side of the ball. That was the thing that bothered me.

"Here's a little story from when he was in the news. I had just come back from vacation. I was working out at a gym. I hadn't seen him since he left the University of Alabama. I went up to him and he almost didn't recognize me- I was bigger than I was now. I told him: "Whatever you doing, don't do it!" But I told him, I didn't agree with what he was doing, but I am with you.

"He was nervous about it. He was trying to justify what he was doing and I gave him an opportunity to tell it to me. We went around the table a couple of times about it, and when it got bad, he called me and said: 'Cuz, I don't know what's going to happen. I negotiated with these people and put myself out here, now I gotta deal with it.

"We were hearing from his old teammates. He started getting the threats. Those were the things that kept him on edge. He would call me and ask me: 'I need somewhere to be.' And he would be with my wife and me since we didn't have kids at the time. He even did that for a while..

"He eventually came back to Alabama and did something that really upset me- the bust in the hotel. He had an episode over here and I told him to really rethink what you're doing. But he felt like something was getting kicked out from under him at the time and that it was self-induced.

"The next thing I hear, he's in California. He tried to hold a couple of jobs. It wasn't working out for him and he was struggling when he came back.

"I was the only member of the family that was in contact with him at the time. He would be like,

"Hey, cuz, I'm just checking in.' It was just a tough time for the whole family. It was just bad all around. I told him you have got to get with the program, but you get what you deserve. A lot of people still feel that way. Most people don't know the inside story and how it really played out. I always felt like, really, it was basically a tug of war with Coach Curry and him really not working out in the way he came to the university in the first place.

"The whole attitude that people had... that he didn't come through the right channels. I thought it was a battle of the Birmingham alums- a Battle of the Machines- against the rest of the Gadsden machine.

'Bobby Humphrey is our guy. Our featured guy is Bobby Humphrey, not Gene. And anybody looking at it has got to say it didn't come right. The biggest group is the Birmingham alums and this is an option that you have to do something with.

"Looking at Gene and how he performed as a running back? Coach Saban... if you look at his program now and compare them, Coach Curry didn't have that.

"Gene resurfaced four or five years ago. And he is trying to go down the right spiritual path- working on doing his ministry. I reconnect with him daily at home. I know he is trying to find some work, and always trying to support himself but it was a struggle- especially when he wasn't working. When you have those kinds of ghosts, and you yourself are paranoid about people around him? I don't know if they were helping or hurting him- you're always guarded.

"One thing you can't change is what you've done. You try to focus on what matters to me. And for me, if I was Gene it would be my daughter and my mom...

"No matter what happens, I tell him to keep moving and go with your heart and it will work out. That has always been a message with the family- keep on moving and do the next right thing."

Todd Clough

"He was just mad at everyone back in the '90s... mad at coaches, mad at everyone. He was just a mad guy. Then, he disappeared and we don't see Gene for a while. I would hear from him every now and then. He lived on streets, under bridges, and overpasses. It was a bad situation.

"He has turned his life around, and finally, he can go where Coach Curry was at. I don't think Curry realized how much he hurt Gene. He scarred him for life. He took his passion and what he was born to do, and he has had to get over it. Whether our passion is soccer or whatever- you're hurt. The divorce rate is high in our country and the passion when one leaves a relationship goes and the other gets hurt. This was like a divorce and Gene got hurt bad mentally. But he has come a long way back.

"Now, he devotes his time to help better somebody else's life. He spoke at my church. He's getting better, but he's real bitter. I had a son get sick, and he called every day. He asked me: 'What can I do to help for your family?' He prayed with me over the phone. He has always been a very caring person. It took him a long time to try to recover. You want to know the truth? A lot of those bad times makes you a better man now that he's gone through it.

"But when it got bad for Gene, everything was real quick.

"He would tell me: 'I'm at the bottom and I can't get out. Three to six months would go by and the phone would ring and it would be Gene. He had to be careful coming into the town where he was raised. Now, he is welcomed back home.

"Gene's all about helping anybody. I have seen him come from the bottom and now he's running the ball back where he needs to be.

"He is a very powerful guy and a powerful presence. He is a good speaker. Thank God I didn't go down that path. But I always thought that he can get through something like this and I waited for that call where something bad happened. He went through drugs, turned his back on his college, and a lot of people. The reason he did is that he got scared, and that meant that much to him.

"What happened in Tuscaloosa hurt him so much- there were things you couldn't coach when he was at rock bottom and not listening out of the trenches. God swooped in and told him that he was going to get back on that winning team doing things he should.

"He is a wonderful guy. He went from chasing the Heisman to the pits of hell. He is now redeemed, and God has given him a second chance. He is making the most of the second chance God has given him.

"When you look back at Gene's situation, life is going to beat you down. Things are going to happen. Somebody is going to steal what you have a passion for. But you can't steal it, unless you let them take your soul and your faith. Even though, it happened, God put Gene back on the winning team.

"The moral- when it's fourth and inches, do you punt or go for it? For Gene, there were no more punts. He went for it, got the first down and got a new life. When he was at bottom, he didn't weigh but 120-130 pounds. He looked terrible. There was nothing else he could do but come up. He had done dug his grave.

"But God wasn't ready for him to enter the grave. There's still work for him to do...

"He started out as a guy that was just unreal and he was built like a rock that could run like a deer. He had the speed and the agility, but he looked like he was 80 years old when he returned. It breaks your heart because he has so much to offer...

"That's how powerful the game of football is in this state, and you don't turn your back on your team. Everybody makes mistakes, people give me some forgiveness and I would ask for them to do the same. This is the new Gene, not the old Gene.

"Take the state of Alabama in football. There are three things you don't talk about- Alabama/Auburn football, religion, and politics. The most powerful of those is football. If you're an Auburn fan, a lot of people may not talk to you. That's how powerful it is. He's saying he made a mistake, but I am trying to get better. Hopefully, hearts will see what he is trying to do.

"People still talk about Gene to this day because of how good he was. His passion was taken from him and now he's doing good things. You pray for folks' hearts not to be (full of) malice and see people are opening up more and more. If you would just see what he is trying to do, everything slowly coming back around for him in his life."

Steve Smith- pastor now in Gadsden at New Destiny Christian Church

"I realized it had been two decades since I saw him. God put it on my heart to invite him to speak after I had talked to his mom. From that day since, I embraced him. I asked him to hold his head up. As many people who were upset, there are more that have accepted him. He has come back to the city of Gadsden and has been a blessing to other children.

"I followed the situation at Alabama with Gene and I knew something was going on behind the scenes. He was too good an athlete to be switched from offense to defense. I followed it because there's no way that should have happened when he had a professional career in his sights.

"I wanted to know what exactly is going on and Gene and I had several discussions about it- I wanted to know what happened. I saw someone make a decision that affected his entire NFL career. Gene had a competitive edge and nature to play somewhere. It wasn't that he chose to play defense. Everyone knew his career was on the other side of the ball.

"I know they were both (Humphrey and Jelks) gifted athletes, and you could tell they both had promising careers. I saw the switch- it didn't make any sense. It was obvious that Gene was being slighted and we didn't know why.

"A lot of what Gene did was out of anger because Gene wanted to play pro ball- he didn't have a plan B. He had ability and the talent to play in the NFL, but when it didn't pan out, it got really nasty.

"His mother has always been in church all of her life. I would communicate with her and ask what was going on with Gene. She would give me updates... speculating he was underground. No one could talk to him personally, but you just wanted to tell him, 'Gene you can do all you can do over there, come on back home. People love you here. I remember I was holding a session called "Can you handle my scars?" at the time and that's why I remember what happened in his life.

"When he came back, I was overwhelmed at the speech he gave. It was a blessing for him and for me as well- I love him and care for him. As of a couple of years ago, for 20 years, we didn't talk at all. That's a long time for a friend, but he had made up his mind. He didn't want to see anybody or talk to anybody.

"Sometimes when we get older, and look back at what used to be, I would collect his write-ups in a scrapbook- as well as mine. There are pictures of he and I together. And it made me think about him a lot. He's just a good friend, not just an acquaintance. I ate dinner at his house and we would tell each other that we love each other.

"He has embraced what he is, and that's hard for people to do. He has accepted that the dreams and goals that he set out for himself as a teenager, those didn't come to fruition. Now it's 'take what I have and the cards that have been dealt.' He has been good at it. You can see that his mind is made up and he's not going back to the old ways. I blessed him with a car, all he needs is an opportunity.

"He never asked me for money. When I found out he was walking back and forth to a job in Atlanta... that was when I gave it to him.

"To better himself in the long run, all Gene needs is an opportunity. He has accepted there are always going to be people who don't forgive him. People can be very unforgiving. He has spoken in Tuscaloosa since and I think that more are embracing than he was focusing on his life at the time than those who are harboring bitterness."

Sam Bryant- Friend and former teammate

"I had heard he was in bad shape- the word was Gene was 'out there,' he's 'doing drugs.' Crack became the drug of the 80's. Typically what they meant, when you were having friends and family who were 'out there' was there was nothing they wanted to have was–dying included- more important than the desire to get that drug. That was my first time hearing that phrase. Most understand the unspoken rule- that the cream rises to the top and people will do what they need to do take care of it.

"And that's part of the frustration in all of this going all the way back to the beginning- people are in denial how they contribute to the process. They feel like they were harmed now that you've done all you've done.

"Gene and I connected about two and a half years ago. It was Coach Saban's second year. Kerry (Goode) had given me Gene's number. We ended up talking for a while, physically, on the ride to Tuscaloosa for A-Day. From the time we exchanged phone numbers- and that was, I think, 2006 to 2007- he just started to reach out to me. He is a really good guy. I could only imagine what he experienced. We use the words gullible and naive. We all have the dream of trusting grown men to play pro football. But when you become a man, it didn't work out however hard you tried. But you can only imagine I tried to do what I could to keep him encouraged.

"The biggest thing now has been to keep him positive. You impart on him a different perspective in the future. He's going to have trust issues. But things in the past...? Others can understand them if you understand them, and you'll know what not to do next time around. If you go with your emotion and shed the beast holding you back, you can step into the next opportunity.

"But back to that A-Day drive- we just laughed like college kids all over again. And that was it. Gene felt he was glad to be back on campus, he was apprehensive about how he would be received. So, we tried to keep it as light as we could.

"There are those who would say... those that feel he violated the brotherhood... they're probably more a better station in life. Until you can walk in a man's shoes, you can't understand why they do what they do. It was about struggle and adversity–he was coping, because he was 'out there.' He didn't have his faculties just trying to survive. The 'cold' of the guys I know that played with Gene is still there, but at the same time there are those that still love him and they understand. They don't take it personally.

"When it comes to the Goodes- Chris and Kerry- I always told folks- one was the heart (Cornelius Bennett says it was Chris) and one was the soul- Kerry. The Goode family embraces everybody. They understand. The guy made a mistake. He did the best he could. He missed a block. He fumbled the ball. It made it easier to give up the ball. But you just don't kick a man when he's down. A man reaches down to help a man when he needs to be picked up- you learned that in team sports.

"It is a testament as to who they are as people- and their parents. They're doing the same for him they want done for their brother or son. It is a chore to keep him positively presented and moving in the right direction. But they are comfortable enough in who they are. They're not compromising, but the question is: 'If I fell what a brother would do...? It's about helping me when I am down, protecting me when I am hurt, and not kicking me.

"I think I have seen him hold onto the resolve that made him the great athlete he was. A part I agree with- the challenge of what he went through- no man or woman is an island. You have to have someone else to help. Gene's challenge from now is to hold onto his faith and belief and just get someone to tell him to do 'this'- whatever 'this' is. It gives him a sense of purpose- and he needs to have someone else's help. He is coping with it better now.

"Gene has gone back to what eased his pain. Gradually and subtly- through all these trials and adversities- you can see the fruits of the efforts. Right now, he can't see them and he moves forward on faith alone. All we can do as friends is try to listen to him and make him understand that you still have to hang in there. You need those teammates around you still after all these years. They're trying to make those blocks for him. One of us, really, can make a block for that one last burst through the hole for him.

"We all send a variation of that message, embracing it when we talk to him. If you carry the ball 30 times, and you've got 40 yards, you're still positive. But you have taken a lot of licks. That's the good thing about football. You get 30-45 seconds to regroup. But you feel every blow you've taken and some before that, if there's time on the clock, you have a chance.

"All you hope and pray at some point, is that people realize we are more similar than we are different. You keep that in our minds we are humans. We are not gods no matter how special we feel we are. Compared to others, we are still the same person.

"We are human with strengths, and as much as we can encourage each other, the better society is. We care about our kids- the least, the last, and the lost is who we do the best for. If we are doing the right thing for the right reason, we eliminate the problems."

Pierre Goode- Friend and teammate from the University of Alabama

"When he was playing, Gene was better off at running back at Alabama, even though he was a good defensive back. I think he would have had a bright future in the pros and I think he would have made some Pro Bowls. I think, with all the competition on the team, he could have held it down and been one of the top five running backs in the country.

"But the coaches made a move for whatever reason. I still think he could have held it down and could have been starting the whole time.

"But I think all of this trickled down into him being very bitter. It made it harder for him to excel and do what was needed there. I think his heart was still at running back and that he may not have had the will to keep going at times.

"I do think that this shows that you can come out of anything. It seems like Gene is slowly coming out of it and once you convince yourself and train yourself to do something, you can accomplish anything.

"I remember once he said, 'With God, he's been blessed.' And I knew he was back to the old Gene. We're all going to make sure he's alright from this moment forward."

Kareem Jones- Co-worker during Gene's days in Atlanta

"There were times you could tell he was upset about decisions he made. You could tell he recognized he messed up, but he was always positive and optimistic. He always made fun of my arms after my workouts at the gym, but he never really broke down. I knew he may have been homeless, but thought he still had some kind of support. He never looked like he was sleeping in a dumpster, but he may have been for all we know.

"He briefly worked at a restaurant called 'Cloud 9'- in the kitchen, maybe for a week or two at that. It was not a long stint. He was always in and out.

"He stopped in Cloud9 sometime in the last two years, and he may have stopped in 2 or 3 times with a lady friend. But if you look at his attitude- it says a lot about an individual. He got down to the bare minimum and fell to the bottom, but he maintained a positive attitude and it says a lot of his strength. Some people, when they face what he faces, go crazy. Some commit suicide. Some go to do drugs, and some other people have it weigh on them heavy to the point of them being unrecognizable. But Gene...? He had a positive attitude maintained the whole time.

"When it comes to Gene, I think the lesson is: be humble and grateful when you have opportunities. Understand at any moment it could be taken away. Stay loyal to your church and faith. At any point, it can be taken way, so just be positive and stay as grounded as you can. You don't want to be like me and have to rebuild my situation- a lot of athletes and kids need to recognize that you still need to maintain what it takes to go up."

Darrin Mayo- Played against Gene in high school, now contracted in the health care industry

"The first time I saw him after all those years, I kinda shook my head- I didn't think it was Gene. After I got reconnected with Gene, and I talked to some of our friends about seeing him- to this day- never forgave him. To this day, there are very little facts and big myths. Gene and I have similar upbringing, but at the same time we had no idea how poor we were.

"We were both from families of strong faith. My dad was a priest, and those men gave us strong moral compasses. I refer to that in times of stress to stay strong – always thinking about going to do what's right. In the long term, it comes out right if I follow that moral compass.

"But when Gene and I reconnected, we would talk about the past more and more. Who would have thought a company would have let a poor kid fly to Los Angeles to meet with folks in New York City to sell a product. We are both thankful to be where we are and experience what we have experienced.

"But starting out, when Gene and I talked it was mostly about Gene struggling and trying to get on the right track. I let him know he has friends he hasn't tapped into to get back on his feet. I have a car repair shop. Gene made a trip, and he had a wheel bearing in bad shape. We did his repair to show him he has friends. It would have cost him more to take it somewhere else.

"My first response about the lesson here...? These old relationships run true. People believe in you if you do the right thing. There are people pulling for you to do the right thing. If you talk to him, there's a lot of misinformation out there today about his story. You see a kid who is poor- most folks think when they make it, everyone else is envious or happy.

"The concept is always that the rich get richer. But, really, there's only two-percent old wealth. 98- percent have earned it. They have worked hard for it. You don't get that for someone if the whole world is pushing against them.

"But the way I told it to Gene, when it comes to his story, was that tempered steel has to go through fire...

"And he said, 'That's what I needed to hear...'

"I think I also told him that same fight that took you when everyone told you that you couldn't...? That's the same fight that will help you get ahead...

"The kids that make it today, the ones especially in the black community and Native Americans – the biggest force against them is their own neighborhood. Gene overcame that.

"I wish we would talk about it more..."

Alex Scarborough- ESPN.com columnist

"Football really is everything to a lot of these guys. There is no Plan B with a lot of them. It's clear how Gene holds on to one decision within a career that he doesn't understand had other opportunities.

When a little part of one dream for an Alabama great goes away, it disrupts their whole life.

"It made him a broken man.

"The big thing, and I get why Gene is upset, is that a lot of athletes in college football lose perspective. They thought, 'I got here. I did this. It should be smooth sailing,' and sometimes it doesn't work out that way."

Bo Wright- teammate at Alabama, now a community activist in Mobile, Alabama

"I want to start out by saying that I love Coach Curry like a father, but I don't think it was a smart move sending Gene to defense. Bobby and Gene were the best running backs in the USA at the time. I just didn't see the need. Why didn't you put any other wide receiver or linebacker back there...? You could have put anybody back there.

"Gene was mediocre as a defensive back and took one for the team! If he wasn't mediocre, they could have put anyone in there to do that.

"I was just asking Gene about it this year- back when he came forward in the 1990's. I didn't know about it because I was in Buffalo with the Bills. To this day, I still have no idea what happened with that situation.

"Gene and I went through the same walk in life. I received a gunshot wound December 12, 1991 by a 13-year old kid. After that, I played indoors with the Tampa Bay Storm and won an Arena Bowl. But when I ended my career, I also turned to a life of the streets- drugs, crack, and all that stuff. It turned into a street life, but God delivered me. It's only fair that I come back and help others.

"I equate drugs with being obese. You don't want to be. But there are people trying to lose weight and don't know how to do it. It's the same with drugs- crack, heroin, alcohol, whatever... people are turned into people they don't want to be. I know I didn't want to be the person I became. I couldn't even manage a five-dollar bill. It told me what to do. People don't know how to be free. I discovered, and Gene did too, that the only way to be free in this life time, is to accept the spirit of God.

"Once we understand the power and that kind of authority, the church is going to take off like a rocket! We are some of the most powerful people in the world at that point. In Genesis 1 and 26, the Bible talks about dominion- the supreme authority in this earth is the same spirit that placed the stars, the moon, and rose Jesus Christ from the death.

"The same spirit resides in us once we're saved. It tells me I am powerful. It's powerful- telling us we don't have to walk around addicted. And it goes to helping people.

"Gene and I are like brothers. Gene and I started touching base frequently ten to twelve years ago going through some things. We pour our hearts out to one another- and when we're feeling a certain kind of way, we call each other. We have free long distance, so we got to bond even tougher than before. Our talks have always been very straight forward. Gene never met a stranger, and neither have I. It's the same kind of kindred spirits. We just clicked.

"It was like we were together all the time, and Lower Gym was the first step in that. We were running backs spending time together in college. We have always been tight, but to find out what he's been through...? It's similar, naturally, we have special kind of bonds.

"Our conversations all this time have been very honest. He was honest where he was, living on the streets, being homeless, and still calling from time to time. There were people talking to me that he was homeless. I would tell those people to give him my number. And it was finally Freddie Robinson who would give him my number...

"With me down here in Mobile, down here on these streets, I'm trying to get my life together. It was just real at that point. He was letting ME know I am not doing well. He would tell me, 'Bo, you gotta get into a program.' I would tell him, 'Gene, you gotta get into a program.' He would make his way to a half-way house, and his life would manifest in the way it was supposed to go. We would stay in contact more and more. He became stronger, and would end up encouraging me, too. It has always been straight forward and honest with the two of us. It has always been a friendship.

But one story that Gene shared with Bo always stuck with him:

'Bo, I was in Atlanta,' Gene told him one day. 'It was cold and raining, and I was dying to get to the other side of Atlanta because the drugs were holding me back. I just started walking. I was up for three days when I came upon an abandoned apartment complex. They were demolishing it. I was tired and cold and I didn't have a coat and jacket. My clothes weren't right, but I climbed into the apartment complex and fell asleep.

'The next morning, the people came to do their job. The building was set to be demolished. But before they were going to knock it down first thing in the morning, one of the gentlemen on the crew came and checked the building out to see if there was anything going on inside.

'I was lying in the building dead asleep.

'It was the grace of God that had that man come inside the building before they knocked it to the ground. I would have been crushed when they had started doing their work, but I was saved.

'Bo, God saved me that day"

"He's a man of God," Bo continues. "Now, he is giving back to the community. So think about those two extremes. God takes him from that extreme to where he is now.

"The overall message...? It has to do with righteousness in my mind. You have to cling to it and do things the right way. Coach Saban says to do things the right way all the time, not some of the time. Do it all of the time...

"I tell my students now, 'Do you realize what the world considers a grown person without education? Get your education now! A lot of people now are in your corner. But if you wake up a grown man, broke, and you fooled round in high school, that's a bad thing waking up grown and broke.

"If you see your name on a cell phone- meaning someone is reaching out to you- there should be training in your mind as a young child to do the right thing all of the time.

"That's the message: Do the right thing all the time, get focused as a young man. We weren't really focused back then. And if I had to say it again and reflect, as we were, and all the messages ringing in our ears went downhill without remembering or learning it, it's like being a surgeon and waking up and you can't use your hands anymore.

"The central message has to be- Do the right thing all the time and I have to prepare myself for the future.

But did Gene violate The Brotherhood by doing what he did...?

"That's a tough call for me... the shoes they put Gene in...? That's some unprecedented stuff. Say someone is an NFL running back and they move him, it didn't violate my brotherhood.

"Others...? It's on them.

"Well, some of those people who haven't forgiven him are the ones who haven't walked in his shoes, and have a career snatched from him the way it was. I'll tell you straight up- he didn't violate it with me.

"I think they ought to pay college athletes anyway."

God said if a man labors, he is to be rewarded. But the issue these days with college athletes, if you ask Gene, is that reward and the level of the reward. At the age of 17, no one told him that he couldn't take gifts and money from college coaches. Hopefully, future student-athletes can learn from the situations

Gene was in when he was in high school and college and proceed with the caution of their years in front of them front and center."

Antonio Langham- Alabama and NFL Defensive Back

The brotherhood means everything. It goes all the way to the creation of the University of Alabama. It doesn't matter when you played. You're there for life. You're always there for each other. And when we need each other, we're there for them.

"It's simple. When you need your brother, you call on them, and they'll be there.

"Did Gene violate 'The Brotherhood' when he did what he did? Some will say 'yes.' Some will say 'no.' Each person will have an opinion on how his situation was. At the end of the day, Gene made a decision based on his feelings and his feelings alone. As a Brotherhood, were we supposed to hate him? We've always been taught that, when we went to Alabama, we are a family. Regardless of what our brother does- right, wrong, or indifferent- that we're supposed to love him. Because that's all we are- a family...

"I didn't hate him or have a problem with him. I don't everyone that played there did. I think there's a different way it could have been handled or a different way he could have handled it.

"Who knows what he was thinking or what was in his mind...? Every man makes his own decision and he has to live with the decision he makes. People think: 'What possessed him to do this?' We don't know. We don't know what he was going through- the anger, the disappointment, the hatred? Who knows? But he played at Alabama, he is my brother, and we couldn't do anything else but love him. WE couldn't find him for the longest time, but we love him just the same.

"He had to look his problems in the eye and realize that his life really isn't that bad. But he is a testament to his character and his upbringing. We knew how his parents raised him. But he found God. And once he found Him, He brought Gene out. And he came out on top. God is the one who brought him through this.

"He wouldn't be the man he is without it."

Hoss Johnson- Alabama and NFL Offensive lineman, Huntsville Parks and Recreation Department (Now Retired)

"You know the old saying, 'FIDO? Forget it and drive on?' I think that's what Gene has done. Gene is installing a new part of his life in God and His beliefs. He has come back to his home town, now, too. That's got to be hard. This is where a lot of it started. I think it tells a lot about his character and how he is willing to face his past.

"It's ironic. This whole situation started with Gene being moved to defense- physically and mentally. He has had to play defense against the charges to this day. He has had to play defense spiritually and against others. It started when he got moved and he got upset.

"The good thing is that it's all behind him. The Brotherhood will support him and, hopefully, they'll help in that. His actions tell you a lot. He apologized. He is trying to make it right. But there are guys who have both and have not supported him since. A lot of us, though, are saying what happened is behind us."

William "Corky" Frost- Auburn booster, now retired

"In nearly every situation in life there are winners and losers. You don't have ties anymore- chess, golf, basketball, and now, college football, there's going to be a winner. Even in most of life's struggles- war, business, and even romance- you usually have a winner and a loser.

"I think the lesson to be learned from the Jelks situation is that there really are no winners. There may be a short-term or temporary winner, but in the long run there are no winners. We accomplished what we set out to do. But the cost was far too much. Most of the people I grew up with were Bama fans, friends and family. I think I lost more than most anybody involved- including Jelks- not my true friends but friends.

"Why?

"Media...

"As an example, people on the inside who actually knew what went on with Eric Ramsey, knew there were no steaks. But that became one of the primary media stories based on three years of taping by Eric & his wife. Even '60 Minutes' admitted in Dudley's (Dudley Perry, the Frost family attorney) office 10 days before the story aired, that they had privately talked with Eric and had gotten him to admit there were no steaks...just taped conversations.

"When Dudley asked what their story was going to be now that the steak story was dead, they replied 'We run it. We have Eric and his wife on tape saying that you gave them steaks on a regular basis and we have too much money invested in production to change now so we go with it,' and they did. Needless to say, my respect for '60 Minutes' tanked.

"You look back in retrospect and you think, 'I should have never taken his first phone call.' That's the truth.

"Right now today, these kids are taken much better care of than they were in the '80s and '90s. They don't go hungry. Back then, they didn't go hungry. But you didn't know that. I mean that you didn't know that he didn't have two fish sticks in his freezer to feed his family for eight days. That's why he needed to borrow $50 for groceries or something like that. You never knew those things.

"I personally wanted to go on '60 Minutes' and deny the tape. A few, who had Auburn's best interest in mind, asked me not to speak on '60 Minutes.' Questions were not scripted and you never know where a live interview is going to wind up with their ability to edit. Did I know that I could end up being the fall guy by not speaking live and defending myself...? Probably. The love for Auburn, or Alabama, can definitely sway your thinking.

"So the people who know that are at Auburn, they love the hell of you. But the folks that don't know what really happened... they sometimes have a totally different opinion of you. Not always, but sometimes.

"And, then, you come over to the other side of this thing...? People who know about the Jelks situation... and they know that John Thrower played a big part in trying to get it off the ground. What a lot those same people don't know is none of the Auburn crowd that I know, even John, influenced Gene to come forward. He had attempted to tell his story several months earlier through a TV station in North Alabama. At that time he was persuaded to give it up.

"I was contacted by an individual from Gadsden & asked if I would get it going. My reply was 'Not in Alabama.'

"All I heard was that John was working on this thing for months. He had actually gone to the SEC office and sat down with Commissioner Kramer. He had tried to talked to Kramer with the copies of the checks (the originals were still in Gadsden), and they were 'going to take care of this.' But nothing ever came of it. John sat up there all day long waiting to see the Commissioner. My understanding is that he never got in.

"Once I decided to get involved, I had two rules: Move it to Georgia and I would personally put no money in the fund. Agreed...? And I was told Gene wanted to come to Georgia. I picked him up at the recreation center on Black Creek and brought him to Atlanta. For more than a week, I moved him from motel to motel to keep Bama from getting to him.

"The Sunday afternoon after I moved him on Friday, I met with John in his office and tried to get copies of the checks. John refused and insisted on going another route. I don't know if he thought we couldn't pull it off in Georgia or what, but my thoughts were then as they are now. Don't mess with Bama in Bama; you'll get hurt.

"Even though we went forward without the checks, John was the target of most of Alabama's legal community as documented in story after story. If you try to do something to hurt Bama in Alabama, with a 60-plus percent fan base, you're going to get lots of negative reaction.

"Once I failed at getting the checks from John, I agreed with (Stan) Kreimer and a couple Auburn people that we needed other evidence or drop it. Jelks came to my office during the next couple of days and created a tape that eventually saved our asses in court.

"If there's one regret, a major regret, of Gene taping from my office, it's Jerry Pullen. Listening to Gene talk to Jerry, I got the same sick to your stomach feeling that I had when I first heard myself on tape with Eric. Jerry was a victim like a lot of people in the Ramsey tapes. One of the nicest people I've ever met.

"Kinda like John... I had more Auburn friends than I knew what to do with. But once the other side convinced Jerry to sue Gene & 99 John Does, being the #1 John Doe, I felt kinda like I was out there on that same island with no ship in sight. That's when your true friends show up. Believe me, most Auburn and Alabama fans are wonderful people if you'll let them be wonderful to you. I received a lot of support in many different ways from both fan bases.

"Alabama fans love what Eric did to Auburn and Auburn fans love what Gene did to Alabama. A lot of people still don't know the truth, and when my name finally came out with it, I wished at that time that we could have gotten John's name out of it. I think Stan Kreimer, Jelks' attorney, eventually got copies of the checks, from John or maybe from Gadsden.

"Me personally, I got hurt more on the Jelks thing more than the Ramsey thing because of being involved in the planning here in Georgia and my time spent with Gene getting it off the ground.

"If I could go back & do it over, if I received a call from Gadsden asking if I would get involved, was I interested in doing something...?

"I would tell my friend from over there that I want to get out of that business. I'd like not to be associated with that."

There are degrees of loss when it comes to this rivalry he feels. There are no real winners...

Back to the media...

"There's a time when you answered a lot of media questions," Frost continues. "You answer a question either admitting something or denying something simply because you want to protect that source or the people you have dealt with. So, it doesn't have to be the exact answer. But when you get under oath, and you do a deposition, you have to tell it exactly. Because the last thing you want to do is to criminalize yourself or perjure yourself by not telling the truth.

"Most of what you read in public records, especially by sports writers, is written with a slant that's best for that particular school they write for. As far as the actual truth, I don't have a lot to claim or disclaim about public records. My involvement with Gene has been well-documented through the years. But if they're going to put some public record out there, put them ALL out there.

"My point is: When Gene went public, just like Ramsey, it blew up all over the country in all your media outlets. Ramsey on '60 Minutes,' Gene on 'Larry King Live...' Court documentation, public records say that Gene was truthful. He had his day in court. Not by his choice, but he did have his day. I personally know that Gene was truthful and Eric, well, Eric was never challenged in court.

"A group of Alabama people and Jerry Pullen sued Gene Jelks & 99 John Does. That was big, real big as a headline in every paper in Alabama and many others across the country.

"Gene was properly defended and prevailed in court. Once Gene's attorney's decided that it was time to end all of the depositions, trips to Overland Park and the NCAA offices, they presented, along with Gene's tape, and asked for a summary judgment. The judge came back two days later and ruled in Gene's favor. At that time, I saw a lot of compassion in Gene that I had not seen up to that point. Gene had counter-sued not long after the original suit was filed. Gene could have asked for damages and probably made life miserable for several people. He didn't and walked away.

"The other side appealed and again Gene prevailed.

"The other side went all the way to the Georgia Supreme Court and again lost to Gene.

"That's all documented in the DeKalb County Court records. However, the coverage of Gene's victories did not get the same coverage as the original lawsuit. I read about it in one of the Alabama papers back in the sports section next to a massage parlor add.

"I think public documentation is fair and public perception is all well and good if it's fairly presented.

"In most instances, it's not done fairly.

"But to summarize, there are no winners... they may think there are, but there are no winners..."

Jerry Pullen- Former coach of Gene's, now working in Knoxville in medical sales...

Jerry admits that, if he still had the opportunity, he would still be a coach. A recent meal with Jerry Glanville in Knoxville reinforced that. When Glanville would address Jerry during lunch, it would always be as "Coach." His job in medical sales is helped by his coaching background and he is still tied to the high school game. Eddie Courtney, long-time and well-respected coach at Knoxville-Farragut is one of his good friends.

He feels really blessed with what he has been able to accomplish in Knoxville. He is coming upon his 34th wedding anniversary with a grandchild on the way.

He always looks back fondly to his time in Gadsden. Pullen says it was a great place to grow up when both mills were up and running. The youth sports there in that time were great as well. When he went to the University of Alabama, those three years were special for him in his life. Getting to work with coaches like Gryska, Bailey, and Donahoo while working with Bill "Brother" Oliver. He looks at what Nick Saban has done there and says it's satisfying for him to see those kinds of results.

He is active in his church and has a Bible study group with two gentlemen named Jerry in it.

"They call me 'Jerry with a Past,' to tell us apart," he says with a laugh. He has been in his current position for 14 years now and enjoys his customers and being a part of their lives. He also has a serious amount of respect for those who work in the medical field these days- knowing the days they put in and what they do during those days to keep us all healthy.

He has made a life for himself in east Tennessee and has moved on from the last quarter-century of life associated with the Southeastern Conference.

"I will say this," Pullen says about the time in the spotlight, "I know now what it's like to have your voiceover played on ESPN and

CNN. And you realize that everyone you see feels like they know you- even though they don't.

"It was a wake-up call, because I knew I wasn't going to get a coaching job and asking myself, 'What am I going to do now?' It's the way I have always tried to face life. You can complain about it, but what are you going to do now? I was fortunate that Sam Hood and David Gilmer, guys who played for me at Alabama, got me on with a company. It took me a little while to figure it out. I have been really blessed since then.

"It's an adjustment. You go from being around guys all the time. And you realize when you get out, that you have to do something else. Now, I recruit customers. It's kinda the same thing I used to do. I love to be a part of their lives now, just having the relationships-watching their kids grow up.

"Gadsden is a blue-collar town and there are some tough kids there. I don't know how it is now, but I do know what these nurses and surgical technicians' lives are like. It has helped me out a lot in that regard.

"I miss the kids and the camaraderie of it and watching a kid coming in with nothing and leaving with a diploma. It's an awesome feeling to see how their lives change from playing and being around college football.

"I tried to get several high school jobs about the same time. I knew I was the best candidate for it, but because of the litigation, I can understand them not wanting to get involved in that at the time. It, pretty much, eliminated me, and I just decided that it wasn't God's Will. So, you move on from there. And what I tried to do in the difference in that is to be involved in my Sunday School, and West Knoxville Youth Sports board. But as far as the coaching part, once you get away from it...???

"I wouldn't go back for any amount of money. I see guys making all this amount of money, but I don't see them having that much of a life. I am glad they're making the money they're making, don't get me wrong. But I still love to watch it and keep up with the guys I know that are still in it. I think Philip Fulmer is getting to that point now, and he is realizing he has a really good deal.

"I think it took me five or six years to get the desire out of me, and now, I wonder at times why I did it. Then, you ask Pullen the same question you as everyone else where the rivalry is concerned:

Are there winners and losers or just degrees of loss...???

"That's the funny thing," Pullen says. "I played my freshman year in college and at that time, if Pat Dye would have offered me a graduate assistantship, I would have gone there. I just got caught in their battle.

"The lawsuit was more about the idea to discredit me- whoever it was paying them. I realize, looking back at some of the questions I was asked in the trial, that there were things in my life that I was very proud of accomplishing. I was in the inaugural class of the Emma Sansom Hall of Fame- one of the first five people on that wall. I look back on it now and I was just a plugger in college.

"Some people thought that I had something against Auburn because I walked on and didn't play all that much. That could not have been any further than the truth! I left and went to West Alabama and played. I was just really glad I was there for Coach Jordan's last year. But Auburn and Alabama isn't even a rivalry- it's a hatred.

"The lesson...??? Football doesn't owe you anything. It didn't owe me anything and it didn't owe Gene anything. I think that would, probably, be the best thing.

"And... you gotta move on..."

Gene Jelks these days

Appendix A
THE LESSON PLAN

Always remember the value of a sign from God.
Gene has…

There are Bible verses that are close to Gene's heart and his struggle along the way to where he is now- especially when it comes to the lessons of the lost son and the Prodigal Son....

And, much like other instances, it came to him in the sign of a visit from a bird- on multiple occasions.

It was a dove that returned to Noah as a sign from God with an olive branch in its mouth, and when the Holy Spirit descended upon Jesus, it was in the form of a dove, a hawk, and an owl.

"I saw an owl once after the death of my aunt Pauline in October of 1995," Gene remembers. "I saw it at the end of the roof at my house. A spirit told me to walk out to the back of the house and stand next to the cooler. And I was thinking, 'I'm not thirsty. Why do I want to go and stand out back next to the cooler?' And there it was… my aunt Annie went with me. The Holy Spirit to me to walk to the left of the cooler and it was right… there…

"My aunt and I went inside and told folks and they all came out and saw it for themselves.

He had another instance of seeing a sign when he was in California.

"I didn't think I was ever going to get to come back to Alabama. I was really stressed out and I thought I could go to California to have all the heat die down. It was on a Sunday afternoon and I was depressed and sad. I was down and all I could think about was the scandal. I told my friend who was with me at the time about birds in the south and a white dove appeared on the roof of her place.

It was thought of as someone from Heaven looking down on everyone who would see the bird. To this day, those in the house are touched by that moment. Whenever they see a dove in public, it is not a personal thought that registers. It is just a reminder that there are signs from Heaven and they need to be paid attention to when you see them.

He had two other instances when he was in a rehab house in suburban Birmingham where an owl appeared in front of him and a hawk came within 15 feet or so of him in Atlanta.

He was sitting in a field in the woods when he received the visit there.

So, as a rule, messengers come from all places. Don't be afraid to receive them and don't be afraid to take their message as part of your own journeys.

Another thought is for women who are having problems in their lives that are similar to those that Gene has experienced first-hand.

So, on a personal note, Gene asked my wife what could be thought of when it comes to addressing addiction and personal challenges to get a female point-of-view. She relayed two stories:

My Grandfather was basically the town drunk in the town he lived in back in Alabama. I'm not sure why – no one has ever said how long he drank or if there was a reason for it. All I really know is that my grandmother finally reached a point where she knew staying with him was no longer a possibility. In the 1940s in small-town Alabama, for her to go through getting a divorce, though, I know it must have been bad. My father has never said that man, whom he addresses as "Mister," hit him or my grandmother (nor did she), but whatever finally made her leave has never been discussed with me. I do know that he did have weekend custody of my dad. He would pick him up, they would go to a bar and my grandfather would go inside and get drunk. My dad would stay outside and "kick rocks" as he tells it – it breaks my heart. I think he was 6 or 7. This went on a while until one day my grandfather arrived

with a woman in the car. He told my dad "This here's Christine – she's your new stepmother."

My dad asked him to please take him home. That was the last time my dad ever saw him.

From all accounts, my grandfather remained with Christine the rest of his life and they had other children. We don't know them – my father has wanted nothing to do with him since that day he asked to go home. I'm sure the rejection by both my grandmother and my dad hurt my grandfather on some level, but perhaps it was the final kick in the butt to get him back on track.

Another woman from my home town was a different story. She was my babysitter and my hero when I was little. She was beautiful – blonde (and her hair was in a perfect early 70s flip!), petite, always tan, always smiling, All-State Band, popular......she was wonderful. Well, one year she went to Panama City for Spring Break....and came back addicted to LSD. She never even was a drinker, which made it so shocking. The story my parents always told me was that someone put it in her drink and one time did it for her. I don't know if that is true or if they were protecting my image of her and knew I'd be crushed to know she took it on her own. That woman went to Auburn about the time we moved there. I knew she was different when she'd come by the house (only to visit – she never baby-sat anymore but I didn't know why at the time). She looked years older than her age – her beautiful face was now red and splotchy. She was so, so thin. I know she dropped out of school a few times.

The worst feeling I had was the day she showed up with her wonderful blonde hair chopped off....then showed us the rest of it. I guess she'd been high and pulled her hair up into a ponytail and then just cut it above the rubber band....she still had the hair in the rubber band with her.

I asked her why she did it – she didn't know why.

She visited periodically while we lived in another Alabama town – I was always so happy to see her. She was still who she was when I grew up and I loved her. Looking back, I see now that my folks always made sure they were close by when she was visiting. I think my dad also tried to keep her in school and made sure all of her financial aid paperwork stayed current. Unfortunately, the LSD pretty much ate her brain and school became impossible.

She moved back to the town I was raised in and became the "ward" of a family friend and they would make sure she had money to live on and would look after her. After we moved back ourselves, we'd occasionally see her riding her bicycle around town, but she rarely visited. Eventually, I got old enough to know what "happened" to her. By that point, she had been in and out of rehab many times and most believed had permanent brain damage from the LSD.

To me, she became a tragic cautionary tale and one I thought about every time I went out. One day, I want to ask my dad what he talked to her about all of those times she visited. I am sure he continued to try and pull her out of the drug abuse and once again be "ours," but the grip was too strong. I never really thought before about how hard that must have been for them – to see what happened to her, to try and help, but still to try and let my sister and I have our illusions about her – all while keeping us safe from her demons. What a tight-rope that had to have been. I'm sure that is what everyone who loves an addict goes through – that balancing act of loving someone, protecting others from them and trying to help. Granted, her case was extreme as you can't really pull yourself back from brain damage, but….

I'd actually forgotten about this until this morning. I walked into the guest room and saw my Polly doll in the chair (the one whose face had faded). Our babysitter appeared at our house one day and gave her to me. At the time, she had on a skirt with lots of pockets and "prizes" in each pocket (I think Monopoly game pieces). My babysitter said her name was "Polly Pockets" and she was just for me. From that day forward, Polly was my favorite doll. Seeing her this morning brought my babysitter's story back –

So…???

The larger lesson that I can think of in these two thoughts…???

I think that every case needs to be addressed individually- with a great deal of patience and care for everyone who could be touched in the situation. Anyone can be in need- and it may not even be someone who may not express the need aloud.

Be sure to ask questions…

Be aware of the situation…

And, just simply, be there- even if the person in need cannot express that need properly. Need and support come in many forms. And you may not even know that you're helping when you are.

Keeping an open mind and an understanding heart will go a long way in making sure the person (or people) you know can make a comeback.

Appendix B
GENE'S VERSES FOR GUIDANCE AND SUPPORT

When Gene was a football star and people would tell him just how good he was, he started to believe them after the "Iron Bowl" performance especially. All of that was before gene came back to Christ. He realizes that God has made us for Himself.

"It's not about me," Gene says now. "It's not about us. It's all about Jesus.'

"I thank God, I can breathe with a sigh of relief for taking evil and turning it around for me for the good," Gene admits. "He promises that no matter what is done to you, He has your back and it could never be undone.

"Your destiny is too great to give up on! Hold on! Keep the faith and keep pushing, no matter what until you reach the finish line. You will never become who God made you to be if you blame others for your mistakes and never forgive. To be blessed by God, stay focused on the one assignment for His Glory and stop trying different things day after day that do not work. Trust the process and keep reaching!

Here are some of them, and hopefully, they will impact you as much as they have impacted him:

Exodus 17-8, 15

Then came Amalek, and fought with Israel in Rephidim

And Moses built an altar, and called the name of it Jehovahnissi:

Luke 15: 9-32 in part

And when she hath found it, she calleth her friends and her neighbours together, saying, Rejoice with me; for I have found the piece which I had lost.
Likewise, I say unto you, there is joy in the presence of the angels of God over one sinner that repenteth.
Jesus continued: "There was a man who had two sons. The younger one said to his father, 'Father, give me my share of the estate.' So he divided his property between them.
Not long after that, the younger son got together all he had, set off for a distant country and there squandered his wealth in wild living.
After he had spent everything, there was a severe famine in that whole country, and he began to be in need. So he went and hired himself out to a citizen of that country, who sent him to his fields to feed pigs. He longed to fill his stomach with the pods that the pigs were eating, but no one gave him anything.
And the act of forgiveness

John 14-6

Jesus answered, "I am the way and the truth and the life. No one comes to the Father except through me.

Psalms 92:8-15 in part

But thou, LORD, art most high for evermore
For, lo, thine enemies, O LORD, for, lo, thine enemies shall perish; all the workers of iniquity shall be scattered.

Proverbs 24-16

For a just man falleth seven times, and riseth up again: but the wicked shall fall into mischief.
Rejoice not when thine enemy falleth, and let not thine heart be glad when he stumbleth:

Jeremiah 5:22

Fear ye not me? saith the LORD : will ye not tremble at my presence, which have placed the sand for the bound of the sea by a perpetual decree, that it cannot pass it: and though the waves thereof toss themselves, yet can they not prevail; though they roar, yet can they not pass over it?

Psalms 84:6
Who passing through the valley of Baca make it a well; the rain also filleth the pools.

Romans 8:28
And we know that all things work together for good to them that love God, to them who are the called according to his purpose.

Philippians 4: 6, 7
Be careful for nothing; but in every thing by prayer and supplication with thanksgiving let your requests be made known unto God.
And the peace of God, which passeth all understanding, shall keep your hearts and minds through Christ Jesus.

Proverbs 28:27
He that giveth unto the poor shall not lack: but he that hideth his eyes shall have many a curse.

Malachi 3: 8-10
Will a man rob God? Yet ye have robbed me. But ye say, Wherein have we robbed thee? In tithes and offerings.
Ye are cursed with a curse: for ye have robbed me, even this whole nation.
Bring ye all the tithes into the storehouse, that there may be meat in mine house, and prove me now herewith, saith the LORD of hosts, if I will not open you the windows of heaven, and pour you out a blessing, that there shall not be room enough to receive it.

1 John 4:4
Ye are of God, little children, and have overcome them: because greater is he that is in you, than he that is in the world.

Ephesians 2-1
And you hath he quickened, who were dead in trespasses and sins;

Romans 10:17
For therein is the righteousness of God revealed from faith to faith: as it is written, The just shall live by faith.

Exekiel 34-26
And I will make them and the places round about my hill a blessing; and I will cause the shower to come down in his season; there shall be showers of blessing.

Jeremiah 33:3
Call unto me, and I will answer thee, and show thee great and mighty things, which thou knowest not.

Habakkuk 2, 1-5
I will stand upon my watch, and set me upon the tower, and will watch to see what he will say unto me, and what I shall answer when I am reproved.
And the LORD answered me, and said, write down the vision, and make it plain upon tables, that he may run that readeth it.
For the vision is yet for an appointed time, but at the end it shall speak, and not lie: though it tarry, wait for it; because it will surely come, it will not tarry.
Behold, his soul which is lifted up is not upright in him: but the just shall live by his faith.
Yea also, because he transgresseth by wine, he is a proud man, neither keepeth at home, who enlargeth his desire as hell, and is as death, and cannot be satisfied, but gathereth unto him all nations, and heapeth unto him all people:

Proverbs 16:7
When a man's ways please the LORD , he maketh even his enemies to be at peace with him.

Jeremiah 17-7
Blessed is the man that trusteth in the LORD , and whose hope the LORD is.

2 Corinthians 5: 5-7

Now he that hath wrought us for the selfsame thing is God, who also hath given unto us the earnest of the Spirit.
Therefore we are always confident, knowing that, whilst we are at home in the body, we are absent from the Lord:
(For we walk by faith, not by sight:)

John 14, 1-4

Let not your heart be troubled: ye believe in God, believe also in me.
In my Father's house are many mansions: if it were not so, I would have told you. I go to prepare a place for you.
And if I go and prepare a place for you, I will come again, and receive you unto myself; that where I am, there ye may be also.
And whither I go ye know, and the way ye know.

Psalms 37, 1-4

Fret not thyself because of evildoers, neither be thou envious against the workers of iniquity.
For they shall soon be cut down like the grass, and wither as the green herb.
Trust in the LORD, and do good; so shalt thou dwell in the land, and verily thou shalt be fed.
Delight thyself also in the LORD: and he shall give thee the desires of thine heart.

Psalms 23, 1-3

The LORD is my shepherd; I shall not want.
He maketh me to lie down in green pastures: he leadeth me beside the still waters.
He restoreth my soul: he leadeth me in the paths of righteousness for his name's sake.

John 8:32

And ye shall know the truth, and the truth shall make you free.

Genesis 22-13
And Abraham lifted up his eyes, and looked, and behold behind him a ram caught in a thicket by his horns: and Abraham went and took the ram,
and offered him up for a burnt offering in the stead of his son.

Exodus 15:26
And said, If thou wilt diligently hearken to the voice of the LORD thy God, and wilt do that which is right in his sight, and wilt give ear to his commandments, and keep all his statutes, I will put none of these diseases upon thee, which I have brought upon the Egyptians: for I am the LORD that healeth thee.

Ezekiel 48-35
It was round about eighteen thousand measures: and the name of the city from that day shall be, The LORD is there.

Jude 1:24
Now unto him that is able to keep you from falling, and to present you faultless before the presence of his glory with exceeding joy

Psalms 23:7
Lift up your gates, O ye princes, and be ye lifted up, O eternal gates: and the King of Glory shall enter in.

Jeremiah 23:6
In his days Judah shall be saved, and Israel shall dwell safely: and this is his name whereby he shall be called, THE LORD OUR RIGHTEOUSNESS .

Isaiah 55:6
Seek ye the LORD while he may be found, call ye upon him while he is near:

Romans 8:37
Nay, in all these things we are more than conquerors through him that loved us.

These verses are just the beginning of what the Bible has done for Gene. He would also have you consult the books of James, Jeremiah, Proverbs, and Habakkuk for further guidance and wisdom in his travels and to assist in yours.

Appendix C

CREDITS/BIBLIOGRAPHY

Reigninggifts.com

Latimes.com, August 2, 2011- Brian Cronin

Sarasota Herald-Tribune, May 3, 1956

Ocala Star-Banner, November 13, 1992- Associated Press: "Ex-Tide Player Says He Was Illegally Paid"

Ocala Star-Banner, November 14, 1992- Jimmy Smothers

Philadelphia Inquirer, September 11, 1987- Jere Longman

Gadsden Times, February 16, 1990- Jimmy Smothers

Tuscaloosa News, January 8, 1990- Hurt and Carroll

Imageshack.us

AL.com

Tuscaloosa News, April 12, 1994- Donna Maltbie: "Police Deny Jelks Was Set Up"

LA Times, August 3, 1995- Gene Wojciechowski

Times Daily Newspaper, December 27, 1992- Associated Press: "Jelks Levels New Allegations"

Gadsden Times, November 15, 1987- Greg Bailey: "Gene Jelks Suffers Knee Injury"

Rolltidefan.net, February 23, 2004: "Dark Side of College Football" interview with Paul Davis

Baltimore Sun, December 28, 1992- Mike Preston: "Bama Probes Ex-Player's Allegations- Sugar Bowl Notebook"

Atlanta Journal-Constitution, July 28, 1994

Atlanta Journal-Constitution, May 2, 1996

Atlanta Journal-Constitution, January 28, 1994- Mike Fish: "Colleges- Mother now supports allegations by ex-Alabama player Jelks"

Atlanta Journal-Constitution, September 1, 1994- JC Clemons: "Documents Allege Jelks Received $37,000 From Lawyer"

Atlanta Journal-Constitution, September 2, 1994- JC Clemons: "NCAA Checks 'Credibility' Of Charges Made By Jelks"

Atlanta Journal-Constitution, October 11, 1994- Mike Fish: "Pullen-Jelks Suit Records To Be Opened"

Atlanta Journal-Constitution, October 14, 1994- Mike Fish: "Jelks' Lawyer Dismissed From Defamation Suit"

Atlanta Journal-Constitution, November 12, 1994- Mike Fish: "Ex-Tide Coach Reveals Booster's $4,000 Loan"

Atlanta Journal-Constitution, November 18, 1994- Mike Fish: "Feudin': DeKalb Defamation Suit Heats Up Ancient Alabama-Auburn Rivalry"

Atlanta Journal-Constitution, June 6, 1995- Mike Fish: "Ex-Tide Assistant's Suit Against Jelks Dismissed"

Atlanta Journal-Constitution, August 3, 1995- Tim Tucker: "Bama Lacked Will To Obey Rules"

Atlanta Journal-Constitution, August 4, 1995- Terence Moore: "Bama Supporters Should Be Angry, But Not At NCAA"

Atlanta Journal-Constitution, October 13, 1993- Mike Fish: "Judge Denies Access To Jelks Recent Financial Records"

Atlanta Journal-Constitution, September 28, 1997- Mike Fish: "NCAA's Secrecy Promise Is Hollow"

Atlanta Journal-Constitution, September 28, 1997- Mike Fish: "A Whistleblower Pays The Price"

Tuscaloosa News, May 16, 2011- Chase Goodbread

Wikipedia.org

Cincinnati Enquirer, October 2, 2003- Rebecca Goodman: "Stanley Kreimer Active In Politics"

Gadsden Times, June 4, 1995- Tommy Deas: "Hearing Concerning Pullen's Suit Against Jelks Monday"

Tuscaloosa News, January 27, 1994- Cecil Hurt Commentary

New York Times, December 31, 1992- Michael Moran: "It's a Showcase Day But What's On Display?"

Tuscaloosa News, April 8, 1994: "Gene Jelks Arrested On Bad Check Charge"

Ray Melick, "Roll Tide Roll," Sagamore Publishing, 1993

AL.com, November 3, 2009- Kevin Scarbinsky: "Chicken Curry and Aggie Stew"

Tuscaloosa News, January 7, 1994- Tommy Deas: "Jelks Linked To Auburn Booster"

The Bible- King James Version- biblegateway.com

Sports-reference.com

CPSIA information can be obtained
at www.ICGtesting.com
Printed in the USA
FFOW02n1636280515
13769FF